EDINBURGH
GRAVEYARD
GUIDE

MICHAEL T R B TURNBULL

*Happy Hunting
in Auld Reekie!*

*Haunting?) Kindest Regards.

Jo

SAINT ANDREW PRESS
1991

First published in 1991 by
THE SAINT ANDREW PRESS
121 George Street, Edinburgh EH2 4YN

ISBN 0 7152 0655 9

British Library in Cataloguing Publication Data

Turnbull, Michael T R B, 1941—
    The Edinburgh graveyard guide
    I. Title
    929.5094134

ISBN 0715206559

Design concept by Mark Blackadder.
Cover photographs by Paul Turner.
Etchings from Cassell's *Old and New Edinburgh*
in 3 volumes, James Grant (1887), from the private
collection of Allan Auld and Geoffrey Warriner.

Printed and **bound** by
Athenaeum Press Ltd, Newcastle upon Tyne.

CONTENTS

FOR
MY MOTHER AND FATHER

ACCESS TO GRAVEYARDS

EDINBURGH CASTLE	Royal Mile (Castlehill) (P)
GREYFRIARS (1562)	Candlemaker Row (CEDC)
ST GILES (1140)	Royal Mile (High St) (P)
CANONGATE (1691)	Royal Mile (Canongate) (CEDC)
HOLYROOD (1128)	Royal Mile (Canongate) (P)
OLD CALTON (1718)	Regent Road (CEDC)
NEW CALTON (1817)	Regent Road (CEDC)
ST JOHN'S (1818)	Lothian Road/Princes St (P)
ST CUTHBERT'S (1127)	Lothian Road (CEDC)
DEAN (1845)	Dean Path (P)
BUCCLEUCH (1756)	Chapel Street (P)
COLINTON (1650)	Dell Road (CEDC)
GRANGE (1846)	Beaufort Road (CEDC)
WARRISTON (1842)	Warriston Gardens (P)
PIERSHILL (1887)	Portobello Road (P)

Thirty-four of the city's graveyards are administered by the City of Edinburgh District Council's Burial Ground Offices (CEDC) at Mortonhall. Those marked (P) are privately owned.

INTRODUCTION

Graveyards are a fascinating gateway into the extraordinarily rich lives of the men and women who have found themselves, by accident or design, in Scotland's capital.

There are those such as the five American Civil War veterans who died overseas and whose bodies were brought back to their native land. There are the unfortunate passers-through suddenly struck by death—such as the scientist Julius von Yellin who was in Edinburgh only to give a lecture. There are those who, like the poet William McGonagall, were born and died in the city. And there are the executed criminals and the Royal children dead before their teens.

In fact there are almost too many colourful characters in Edinburgh's graveyards to do all of them justice in this book. Nor can we do justice to the rich assortment of graveyards and burial grounds which have evolved in and around this splendid capital city. Notable exclusions include Rosebank, Mount Vernon, Craigentinny and Morningside.

I hope that you enjoy the final selection which has tended to include churchyards and cemeteries nearer the city centre. The choice is practical as many of them are within walking distance of each other.

However, a word of caution to the visitor—some of the graveyards of the city present formidable obstacles, like head-high weeds or danger from only too real human spectres lurking in the ruins of long-forgotten tombs. For safety's sake, do not walk alone!

Michael T R B Turnbull 1991

EDINBURGH CASTLE

The spectre of death hovers over the Castle. It started perhaps in the mists of the Dark Ages when it is said that the old 'Maiden Castle' (as it was once known) held the graves of many young girls.

Although the Castle was occupied since the Bronze Age, only a few burials have been found there. There was one body, thought to have been that of the young Earl of Douglas lured to his death in the banqueting hall in 1440; and a number of muscular skeletons (probably part of Cromwell's army) discovered very recently. The only cemetery in the Castle is for the army dogs buried in sorrow by their masters.

On the Castle Esplanade, where many a soldier died in siege or in defence (from the siege of Donaldbane in 1093 to the invasion of the Earl of Hereford in 1544), where 300 witches were burned between 1479 and 1722, there is only one formal grave—that of the Ensign **CHARLES EWART** (1769-1846) (top right corner of the Castle Esplanade, before you enter the Castle itself).

A block of grey Norwegian granite,

placed there in 1938 by the Royal Scots Greys, marks the grave and a carved stone is set in the ground behind.

In 1815 more than 600 men took part in the battle of Waterloo, during which the charge of the Union Brigade took place, coming to within 200 yards of Napoleon himself!

Sergeant Ewart (later commissioned to Ensign) of the Royal North British Dragoons, described his capture of the Imperial Eagle standard of the French 45th Regiment of Infantry (from which the eagle badge of the Royal Scots Greys is taken): 'It was in the first charge, about 11 o' clock. I took the eagle from the enemy. He and I had a hard contest for it…

'Next I was attacked by a foot soldier

EDINBURGH CASTLE in the time of ENSIGN EWART

who, after firing at me, charged me with his bayonet but he very soon lost his combat. I parried him and cut him down through the head. That finished the contest for the eagle. I took it into Brussels amid the acclamation of all who saw it.'

Ensign Ewart was born in the Borders and died in bed in Manchester at the age of 77. In 1937 his burial place was found in a contractor's yard in Salford and his remains reinterred in the Castle Esplanade.

The Scottish United Services Museum at the Castle holds a number of articles associated with Ensign Ewart: the sword he carried at Waterloo; his Waterloo medal; the watch he bought in Paris; his silver snuff-box and the coatee he wore in the Veteran Brigade.

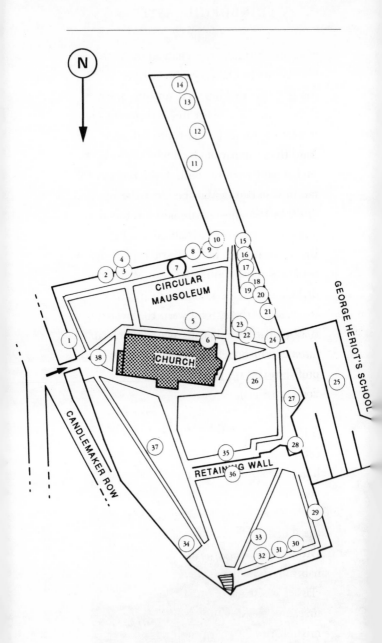

N

CIRCULAR
MAUSOLEUM

CHURCH

GEORGE HERIOT'S SCHOOL

CANDLEMAKER ROW

RETAINING WALL

GREYFRIARS CHURCHYARD

GREYFRIARS

Your first glimpse of Greyfriars Kirk will probably be from the bronze statue of the faithful Skye terrier 'Greyfriars Bobby' ('*from the life just before his death*') at the junction of Chambers Street, George IV Bridge and Candlemaker Row. He sits patiently on his dark granite fountain, the drinking-well, unhappily, now quite dry.

Across the road from you is Greyfriars Bobby's Bar with a penny-farthing bicycle fastened to its rugged stone front and the profile of the wee dog in black above the door.

You go into the churchyard round the side of Greyfriars Bobby's Bar, up uneven cobbles, under an old glass lantern fixed high overhead. Already a sixth sense warns you that this is a place of ancient mystery.

Where you stand was once the site of the church and monastery of the Franciscan Order (the 'Grey Friars' wore a brown habit: in those days the colour brown was classed as a shade of grey). The Franciscans first came to Edinburgh in 1447 as medical missionaries for poor people who were sick. At the Reformation they fled to the Continent.

In 1562 the garden of the Greyfriars was given to the Town by Mary Queen of Scots as an overflow cemetery to relieve the overcrowding in the churchyard of St Giles, the parish church of Edinburgh. Between then and 1900 nearly 100,000 people were buried in the churchyard.

Hugo Arnot, writing in 1778, records that 'the graves are so crowded upon each other that the sextons frequently cannot avoid, in opening a ripe grave, encroaching upon one not fit to be touched. The whole presents a scene equally nauseous and unwholesome.'

To add to the overcrowding, when St Giles was being restored in 1879 several tons of human bones from unmarked graves in the middle of the church were removed and reverently reinterred at Greyfriars.

You may be surprised to hear that the location of many graves is unknown. In 1603 the Town Council had ordered all gravestones to be removed: thus the earlier graves in Greyfriars were marked only with wooden numbered posts.

And since burial records were not kept until 1658, the exact location of the graves of a number of famous people is not known and probably never will be.

The Kirk is a giant barn shooting into the sky. On the east wall, facing you, the bulging rib-cage of a skeleton prances, swinging a scythe and holding the Book of Destiny (you can almost hear the skull cackling). Sharp surgical knives and scissors hang on each side, tied with bows. Ignore the quivering skeleton if you can. Turn immediately to your left past the brown and gold noticeboard which glistens with the names of the famous dead. If you listen carefully you can almost hear a low murmur of many voices from beneath your feet.

The first grave to the left is the imposing monument to [1] **JOHN MYLNE** (1611-67), the sixth Royal Master Mason in his family. Above, a heraldic shield is gripped by two beefy men. A dragon roars below. Under it a contented winged soul spreads its feathers.

Mylne was the fourth John to be a Master Mason from a family who served seven successive kings. Ironically not one of the Mylnes was ever knighted for his services to Scotland.

John Mylne designed the Tron Kirk and built part of Heriot's School (where a fine statue of him presides over the quadrangle). Mylne was not only a builder, he also represented Edinburgh in the Scottish Parliament.

The carved cloth bearing the main inscription—'*Great Artisan, grave Senator, John Milne*'—is framed by the ferocious heads of monsters (perhaps a clue to

Mylne's nightmares?) Two ornate pillars on either side trumpet epitaphs and commemorative verse.

According to the inscriptions Mylne was remarkably handsome, honest, pious and everywhere respected. But the picture you get from his tomb tells another story: skulls, an hour-glass and crossed torches burning upside down speak of the fear and pain of death which haunted Mylne and all the people of Edinburgh in his day.

Shaking off the shiver tingling your spine, walk slowly up the path as it swings right. At the sixth windswept walled grave is a burnished plaque dedicated to the memory of [2] **ROBERT SIBBALD** (1641-1722), Physician to Charles II and founder of Edinburgh's Royal College of Physicians, King's Geographer in Scotland and first Professor of Medicine at the University of Edinburgh.

The good doctor was a bit accident-prone. On one occasion he was coming out of the close at his home, off to see a sick child, when his spurs locked together and, slipping on the wet cobbles, he tottered forward and fell headfirst against the side of the stair. On another occasion he was accidentally hit over the head by a golfer making a stroke on Leith Links.

But accidents did not prevent Robert Sibbald from continuing his tireless work for the world of medicine. He helped found the now Royal Botanic Garden when he planted one of Edinburgh's first public gardens for medicinal herbs—on the site of the present Waverley Station booking office.

In Sir Robert Sibbald's day the world of learning was smaller and it was possible for one man to have a diversity of jobs and achieve so much in one lifetime. The influence of this pioneering Scottish doctor (who had studied his medicine in Holland and France) was enormous. Today his place of burial is open to the skies.

Tread warily past the next walled grave to the ten-pillared stone canopy over the last resting place of {3} Commissary **CLEMENT LITTLE** (*d* 1580) and his brother {4} the Lord Provost **WILLIAM LITTLE** (*d* 1601).

They were two of the three founders of Edinburgh University. Clement Little, an advocate, left 300 books as a generous foundation for the Edinburgh University Library.

Four grim women (noses missing and one headless) stand on guard over the roof. The story once went round that they were four cruel daughters who poisoned their father (now to be seen resting in his tomb). This was a colourful and widely believed way of explaining the eerie-looking monument. The mysterious female figures on the roof seem to threaten the man lying below.

But in reality the disturbing statues are far from evil. They are the virtues— Justice, Mercy, Faith, Love: the good qualities that the Little brothers wanted people to remember them by.

Justice has her eyes blindfolded. One hand grips a sword, the other holds weighing scales. Another statue wears a laurel crown and clenches squirming snakes in her hand. The weather has not treated them kindly, but they stand erect and silent sentinels on the roof.

Under this canopy a plump, badly-dressed man (William Little) casually rests his head by one elbow on a tasselled cushion, as if taking a nap after supper.

Now leave the safety of the path for a moment. Make for the two heavy black iron 'mortsafes' (burial security cages) beside the church, designed to stop those vultures of the night—the grave-robbers (or 'Resurrectionists') looking for fresh corpses to sell for medical research.

Getting bodies for teaching anatomy was always difficult. As early as 1505 the Town Council allowed the College of Surgeons the body of one criminal each year. But this was not nearly enough— anatomical dissection was seasonal; it could only be practised in the winter when bodies could be kept cold. In the summer putrefaction set in quickly.

In February 1678 four gypsies called Shaw (a father and three sons) were hanged and thrown into a pit together in the Greyfriars churchyard. On the following morning the body of the youngest son, aged 16, was seen to be missing. Some thought he might have revived under the shallow pile of earth, having been hanged last and first cut down. But it was strongly suspected that his body had been stolen from the grave by a surgeon.

Over the next 30 years Greyfriars (the chief burial ground in Edinburgh at the time) saw more and more graves robbed by doctors' apprentices. They worked with great secrecy. In those days no one but a grave-robber would dare to go into a churchyard after sunset.

By 1694 the corpses of those who died in the correction house, or the bodies of foundlings who died at the breast, were handed over to surgeons for dissection. At the Royal College of Surgeons today you can still see a skeleton and dissection by Professor Alexander Monro *Primus* and Dr Archibald Pitcairne.

Outside Britain the Resurrectionists were almost unknown. In other countries a reasonable supply of bodies was available legally.

In May 1711, the Royal College of
Surgeons protested that 'of late there has
been a violation of sepulchres in the
Greyfriars Churchyard by some who most
unchristianly have been stealing, or at
least attempting to carry away, the bodies
of the dead out of their graves'.

Ten years later the College of Surgeons
ordered the insertion of a clause of indenture
for apprentices, forbidding them to take
part in the theft of bodies from graves.

But very little changed and in 1725
the people of Edinburgh gathered in the
streets to protest at the disgusting trade in
human flesh. They went to Professor
Monro's school of anatomy and smashed
the windows, putting the fear of death
into the doctors and their apprentices.

In 1742 the body of Alexander Baxter
(who had been buried in Greyfriars
churchyard) was found in a house next to
the shop of a surgeon called Martin Eccles.
The Portsburgh drum was seized and
beaten through the Cowgate. The interior
of Eccles' shop was demolished, windows
in the homes of other surgeons were
smashed and the riot was put down only
with great difficulty. Eccles and some of
his apprentices were taken to court, charged
with the offence of being accessory to the
lifting of bodies, but the case had to be
abandoned because of lack of evidence.

Sir Robert Christison gives a detailed account of the grave-robbers' techniques: 'The time chosen in the dark winter nights was for the town churchyards from six to eight o'clock, at which hour the churchyard watch was set and the city police also commenced their night rounds.

'A hole was dug down to the coffin only where the head lay—a canvas sheet being stretched around to receive the earth and to prevent any of it spoiling the smooth uniformity of the grass.

'The digging was done with short flat, dagger-shaped implements of wood, to avoid the clicking of iron striking stones.

'On reaching the coffin two broad iron hooks under the lid pulled forcibly up with a rope broke off a sufficient portion of the lid to allow the body to be dragged out. Sacking was heaped over the whole to deaden the sound of cracking wood. The body was stripped of the grave-clothes which were scrupulously buried again. It was secured in a sack and the surface of the ground as carefully restored to its original condition—which was not difficult as the grass over a fresh-filled grave always shows sign of recent disturbance. The whole process could be completed in an hour.'

Between the two mortsafes in the churchyard is a large flat gravestone set into the grass. Here lies Lord President [5]

DUNCAN FORBES of Culloden (1685-1747), a dragon on the helmet of his coat of arms poised above three muzzled bears and unicorns.

Forbes was born on the family estate at Culloden near Inverness. As a law student he was a fierce drinker and gambler—he and his brother were known as the greatest boozers in the North. At his home—Culloden House—casks of claret were emptied by the pailful and the massive dining table was stained red with wine.

When Forbes' mother died, the funeral party was so intoxicated that they arrived at the graveside without the body!

Forbes became a Member of Parliament, and in 1737 Lord President of the Court of Session. He began his career by making the Scottish legal system more efficient.

During the Jacobite Rebellion Forbes sided with the Hanoverian King, but after the battle of Culloden he saw to it that the prisoners were tried not in England (where they would have little chance of a fair trial) but in Scotland. He opposed any over-ruling of the Scottish Court of Session by the House of Lords in cases of forfeiture of estates, as this would have been against the Treaty of Union. He objected to the Disarming Act of 1716 which would have made it unlawful for Highlanders to carry weapons of any kind.

After the Porteous Riots, when the English Parliament was determined to strip Edinburgh's Lord Provost of his office, abolish the Town Guard and knock down the Netherbow Port, Duncan Forbes, a true patriot, stood firm for the honour of his country.

So powerful and respected did he become that he was known as 'King Duncan', but he was also called 'one of the greatest men that Scotland bred, as a judge, a patriot and a Christian'.

Proceed with caution towards the end section of the church wall in front of you. Between the last two buttresses are eleven memorial stones set into the wall. In the middle is that of the cheery poet and publisher [6] **ALLAN RAMSAY** (1686-1758):

Tho' here you're buried, worthy ALLAN,
We'll ne'er forget you, canty Callan,
For while your Soul lives in the Sky,
Your GENTLE SHEPHERD ne'er can die.

Ramsay, Lanarkshire-born, served his apprenticeship as a wigmaker. He was a chubby little man with an ugly face, full of fun and amusing conversation.

In 1712 he opened his own wig shop and founded the Easy Club. His next business was at the sign of the

ALLAN RAMSAY

Mercury on the sunny side of the High Street. Six years later he published his first book of poems and then in 1724 his *Tea Table Miscellany*, a collection of Scots songs and ballads.

Ramsay then set up a bookshop at the end of the ramshackle Luckenbooths beside St Giles and opened a lending library —it was the first one in Britain.

The first regular professional theatre in Edinburgh was his next project. This was opened in 1736, but closed down by the bigoted magistrates soon after.

His final home was an octagonal villa on the north side of the Castlehill, the 'goose-pie' at it was affectionately known.

When the Jacobites captured Edinburgh in 1745, Ramsay, a secret Jacobite sympathiser, moved out of the town and his house was used by Prince Charlie's men to take pot-shots at the Castle.

Now turn away from the church to the tall gloomy domed monument with a mysterious urn on its roof, beside the tomb of the Little brothers. Walk slowly over the grass towards it between two menacing green obelisks.

Already there is a faint sense of unease in the air, for this is the tomb of [7] Sir **GEORGE MACKENZIE** (1636-91), better known as 'Bluidy Mackenzie', the hanging judge.

Mackenzie boasted that he had never lost a case for the King, but he also worked to prevent the cruel persecution of so-called 'witches'.

His opinion of heretics was that 'it fares with them as with tops, which, as long as they are scourged stay upright and run'. He had a violent temper, an insolent manner and a cutting tongue. In court he once threatened to take a Covenanter's tongue out with a pair of pincers.

Yet Mackenzie had positive sides to his character—he wrote a pioneering legal work and gifted 1500 books to the Advocates Library (which he founded in 1680). This formed the basis of the present National Library of Scotland.

His monument is gloomy but attractive. Delicate flowering columns separate alcoves shaped into scallop shells. These are the traditional badges worn by pilgrims to St James' shrine in Compostella, Spain. For Mackenzie, life was a long journey towards God and forgiveness.

In the alcove to the right, you can see where forgotten schoolboys long ago carved alphabets into the stone. The solid oak door to the tomb is pierced by two rusty iron grilles, fragile as lace. Peep through them into the shadowy

'BLUIDY MACKENZIE'S' TOMB

heart of the tomb and you see still more scallops inside, scooped out of the stone. Rattle the lock and shout the 'dare' of the George Heriot's schoolboys over the centuries: *Lift the sneck and draw the bar: Bluidy Mackenzie, come out if ye daur!*

Today there is no longer a sneck and a bar—only a stout padlock.

A Clerk of Police, J W Weston, who inspected the interior of the Mackenzie tomb in 1897, recorded that he 'saw and touched the actual hand of Sir George Mackenzie'.

The next grave is in relief—plain and simple—it has only the engraved black letters which record the name of [8] **PATRICK MILLER** of Dalswinton (1731-1815). It is open to the elements and unmarked but for the carving above the lintel.

Miller, Glasgow-born, was a director of the Bank of Scotland, but his hobby was machines. He was a shareholder in the Carron Ironworks, helped improve the quality of their cannons and is supposed to have been involved in the invention of the deadly *carronade*.

A lot of his spare time was spent in Leith improving the way ships were designed and built. He believed that the steam-engine could be used to power boats and in 1788 he tried out his steam-powered vessel beside his estate on Dalswinton Loch in Ayrshire. Among the passengers were the portrait painter Alexander Nasmyth and the poet Robert Burns who was a tenant there.

Walk on with a fresh step to the final wall monument to your left. It is to members of the Siddons family—[9] **HENRY SIDDONS** (1774-1815) and his wife [10] **HARRIOT** (1783-1844).

Henry Siddons was the eldest son of the great actress Sarah Siddons (1755-1831). He appeared at Covent Garden for the first time in the play 'Integrity' in 1801 and eight years later took over Edinburgh's Theatre Royal in Shakespeare Square (now the site of the General Post Office) until his death. His wife was a beautiful woman and a fine actress. She took over the theatre after her husband's death, its greatest success being Sir Walter Scott's 'Rob Roy' presented in 1819.

Now you approach gates marked 'The Covenanters Prison'. This was for some time thought to have been the place where 1200 defeated Covenanters were held in 1679, but the real site was on the Forrest Road side of the churchyard on a part of land now built over. The part of the church-yard beyond the locked gates was not used for burials until 1705. If the gate is locked, the key can be obtained by prior arrangement with the burial ground authorities.

Now go through the gate. At the eighth plot on the left, halfway down, walk through a gate in a low wall armed with railings. Facing you, below a higgledy-piggledy red brick wall, is the white marble plaque to the 'Father of Modern Geology' {11} **JAMES HUTTON** (1726-97).

Living in Edinburgh all his life Hutton was fascinated by the tortured, twisted rocks of the ancient volcano in the Castle Rock, and most of all in Arthur's Seat and Salisbury Crags jutting out of the earth high above the Queen's Park.

But the love of Hutton's life was chemistry. He began as an apprentice in a lawyer's office, but instead of getting on with the drudgery of copying legal papers, he amazed and amused his fellow-apprentices with his chemical experiments.

He soon gave up the Law and studied medicine in Edinburgh, Paris and Holl-and, graduating as a doctor in 1749.

Then Hutton was left a small property in Berwickshire. He began to experiment with new methods of farming and set up a business making salt from coal-soot. He went to England to look at advanced farming methods and became equally fascinated by soil and rock formations.

In 1785 he read the outline of his

Theory of the Earth to the Royal Society of
Edinburgh. This came as a bombshell
because in it he contradicted the accepted
view that the earth had been formed by
the action of the sea. Hutton proved that
it was the action of fire which had shaped
the earth's crust, and he used detailed
studies of the rock formations of Salisbury
Crags to back up his theory.

For a scientific revolutionary Hutton
was a quiet man. He never married and
lived with his three sisters.

Further down on the opposite side of
the path lies Hutton's friend and contem-
porary [12] **JOSEPH BLACK** (1728-99),
Professor of Chemistry.

Black was born in Bordeaux where his
father was a wine merchant, but he was
educated in Belfast and trained as a doctor
in Glasgow.

In 1750 Black came to Edinburgh
where he discovered carbonic acid and then
returned to Glasgow as Professor of Chemistry to discover latent heat. This opened
the way for James Watt to improve the
steam-engine. Black was appointed a
Professor at Edinburgh in 1766.

He was a calm, unexcitable man. Any
stress or strain would result in him spit-
ting blood. But his easy temperament and
pleasant smile meant that he had a lot of
friends. Like Dr Hutton he never married.

His 20 foot high monument is similar to that of Adam Smith in the Canongate churchyard. Fine strips of stone radiate from the centre, beams of light from a shining mind. On each side are the twisted snakes of the medical profession, while in the centre a bearded head forms the keystone of the arch—this is not a portrait of Dr Black but a symbol of his powerful, wide-ranging mind.

Further down on the same side, in the third burial-plot from the end, is the grave of {13} James Burnett, **LORD MONBODDO** (1714-99), an unmarked grave within the family enclosure of

Patrick Grant, Lord Elchies. As a young man Monboddo loved the theatre and dancing, particularly the minuet (dressed in his white velvet suit). He was late described as 'rather like an old stuffed monkey'. Summer and winter he would get up early and take a cold bath. Before going to bed at night he used to cover himself in a cream made of rosewater, olive oil, aromatic spirit and Venetian soap.

LORD
MONBODDO

At the battle of Sherrifmuir he was on horseback when he came upon an English officer who had been stunned by a fall from his horse. Monboddo rode up to him and the officer said, 'Sir, I am your prisoner'. 'No,' answered Monboddo (seeing other English troops approaching), 'I am *your* prisoner.' 'If that is so,' said the officer, 'get off your horse and I will protect you' —and Monboddo was escorted to safety.

Monboddo had strange ideas for his time—he believed that all human babies were born with tails like monkeys and he pestered midwives to be allowed to watch women giving birth to prove his point. In this way he was a forerunner of Charles Darwin (Darwin himself was partly trained at Edinburgh University).

Buried beside Lord Monboddo is his daughter {14} **ELIZA BURNETT** (1766-90)—one of the most attractive and intelligent women of her day.

When Robert Burns first met her at one of Lord Monboddo's famous suppers at the Monboddo home in the Canongate, he wrote: '*Fair Burnett strikes the adoring eye, Heav'n's beauties on my fancy shine*'.

In spite of many offers of marriage, Miss Burnett chose to look after her father. She died from consumption at 24. Burns composed her epitaph: '*Thy form and mind, sweet maid, can I forget? In richest ore the brightest jewel set!*'

Returning to the main part of the churchyard, first on your left is the newly-restored mausoleum of the Adam family,

with its bust of {15} **WILLIAM ADAM**
(1689-1748), affectionately known by his
family as 'Old Stone and Lime'. This is the
work of three of his sons—Robert (aged
19), James (17) and William (9).

Not far from Greyfriars at the opposite
end of Chambers Street was the town house
of the Adam family (they were originally
from Kirkcaldy in Fife). Across the Bridges
is Infirmary Street, once the location of
the first Royal Infirmary which William
built in 1747. The richly-carved Drummond Scrolls and four pillars from Adam's
Infirmary were re-erected in Redford Road
in 1884 after the demolition of the building, while the ornate gates still stand not
far off in Drummond Street. The statue of
George II as a Roman emperor which
adorned the front of the old building can
now be seen outside the present Royal
Infirmary.

Other buildings worked on by William
Adam include Hopetoun House, The
Drum at Gilmerton, the Town House in
Dundee and Robert Gordon's College in
Aberdeen.

William Adam was a many-sided man,
setting up breweries, introducing strong
ale (*barley-bree*) into Scotland and opening
Dutch-tile factories which roofed half of
eastern Scotland.

Beside the Adam tomb is the almost

equally resplendent tomb of [16] Principal
WILLIAM ROBERTSON (1721-93),
chiselled ridges of stone shining out over
its arch in laserbeams of light.

Robertson was a minister, a historian
and Principal of Edinburgh University. He
was partly responsible for what became
Old College and was a founder member of
the Royal Society of Edinburgh, a meeting
place for the finest minds in Scotland.

The next curved headstone is that of
[17] **WILLIAM SMELLIE** (1740-95).
Smellie was born in the Pleasance and
trained as a printer. In his spare time he
attended Edinburgh University, indulging
his passion for botany. He was so know-
ledgeable in that subject that when the
Professor was absent, Smellie was appointed
to lecture in his place.

In 1765 he set up in business on his
own as a printer and edited the first edition
of the *Encyclopaedia Britannica* in the last
three years of his life.

It was Smellie who printed the Edinburgh edition of the poems of Robert
Burns and introduced him to the famous
Crochallan Fencibles (an exclusive drinking
club) at Dawnay Douglas' tavern in Anchor
Close next to Smellie's printing house. To
this day the stools from the print shop can
be seen in the Lady Stair Museum.

Two graves further on is the pointed

headstone of [18] **ALEXANDER
MONRO** *Primus* (1697-1767), Professor
of Anatomy for 34 years, and his son [19]
ALEXANDER MONRO *Secundus*
(1733-1817) who held the same post for
44 years.

Monro Primus was a brilliant
anatomist who became a professor at the
age of 21 and gave the Edinburgh School
of Medicine its international reputation.

He was in attendance at the Battle of
Prestonpans, caring for the wounded and
eventually died from pelvic cancer after a
long and painful illness.

Monro Secundus was the finest
physician of the Monros, with an extensive
practice. Among his anatomical researches
he discovered the small opening in the
brain now known as the 'foramen of
Monro'.

Facing you over the wall are the
delicate silver and grey turrets of George
Heriot's School, visible over the writhing
black decoration of the curious family
grave of the [20] **CHIESLIES of DALRY**
built in 1679. Two noseless women on
each side pray with desperate clasped
hands, tiny weathered angels holding a
hat over a seated scholar, while the bony
figure of Death dances away from the stern
finger of God emerging from a cloud.

Buried here are the parents of John

Chieslie, the man who murdered Lord
President Lockhart in 1689.

The story goes that Lockhart had
presided in court over a dispute between
Chieslie and his wife and ordered him to
pay a living allowance to her. In revenge
Chieslie, who had a violent temper, loaded
his pistols on Easter Sunday 1689 and shot
Lockhart in the back.

Chieslie was tried and sentenced to
death the next day. Tied to a wooden cart
he was dragged through the streets to the
Mercat Cross, while the crowd pelted him
with stones and pieces of metal. His right
hand was cut off and then he was hanged
in chains until his body rotted.

His relatives came secretly, took down
the body and buried it at Dalry. From this
time the Chieslie manor house at Dalry
gained a reputation for strange unnatural
apparitions, hauntings and the smell of
fear. In the nineteenth century a skeleton
was discovered under an old summerhouse
in the garden. The right hand was missing
and a pistol was tied around its neck.

The grave of [21] **WILLIAM CAR-
STARES** (1649-1715) has two grey
corinthian pillars of eroded orange-pink
sandstone. Carstares was Glasgow-born,
the son of a Covenanter. When his father
was forced to escape to Holland, William
followed to study in Utrecht. There he met

William of Orange who employed him as a spy in Britain.

Carstares was imprisoned at the Edinburgh Tolbooth in 1683 and was tortured with the thumbscrews and the hated 'boots'. Eventually he was released and went back to Holland.

When the Revolution took place in 1688, he persuaded the new King William to introduce the presbyterian system of Church government into Scotland. In 1703 he became Principal of the University of Edinburgh.

Walk on diagonally towards the back of the church to the triangular plot of roses between the paths. As you go, you pass the simple slabstone of [22] **NEIL GOW** Jr (1795-1823). His father, the more famous [23] **NATHANIEL GOW** (1766-1831) is also buried there. Nathaniel was born near Dunkeld, son of the famous violinist Neil Gow who taught him to play the fiddle. At 16, Nathaniel became one of His Majesty's Trumpeters for Scotland and later succeeded his brother William as conductor of McGlashan's Band which he directed for 40 years. Between 1799 and 1824 he published six highly popular collections of reels and strathspeys.

Nathaniel was a favourite with George IV (when the Prince of Wales) and was often asked to play for his private parties.

Neil Gow Jr died before his father. He was a talented composer and worked with his father as a music-seller. He composed the tune 'Bonnie Prince Charlie'.

Turn left when you reach the path and walk towards Heriot's school. As you pass, a small pink granite stone on the left of the path records that the lawyer [24] **WALTER SCOTT,** WS (1729-99)—father of Sir Walter Scott—and other members of the Scott family are buried close by. Scott himself was born near the end of Chambers Street and later lived in George Square. His father was an elder at Greyfriars Kirk.

Approach the gates of the School and then take the last path on your right. In the seventh plot on the right under a large tree is the resting-place of [25] **WILLIAM CREECH** (1745-1815), bookseller, publisher and Lord Provost. Creech took over Allan Ramsay's premises in the Luckenbooths. There all the brains of Edinburgh assembled, like bees round a honey-pot, to argue or gossip. Creech's breakfast parties were highly popular with the élite of Edinburgh.

Although Creech printed the works of Adam Smith, David Hume and Robert Burns, he angered the poet by holding back some of the money from the sale of his poems. Burns duly took a swipe at him:

A little pert, tart, tripping wight
And still his precious self his dear delight;
Who loves his own smart shadow in the streets
Better than e'er the fairest she he meets.

Return as you came, back through the arch. Turn first left. As you do so you see diagonally to the right the striking memorial to **[26] GEORGE BUCHANAN** (1506-82) some 26 paces away, his bronze head sheltering into the stone, cap on head and fur collar round his neck.

Sir Robert Sibbald the physician records that 'the skull of George Buchanan (which is more than usually spherical and so thin that the light shines through it) was de-interred from the grave and is now preserved in the library of the University of Edinburgh'.

Buchanan was Stirling-born, a relation of George Heriot. After training and teaching in Paris, Buchanan returned to Scotland as tutor to the illegitimate son of James V.

He was imprisoned by Cardinal Beaton for writing poems criticising the Roman Catholic Church, but managed to escape while his gaolers were asleep, reaching Bordeaux in France where he became a professor of Latin.

Another teaching post followed in Spain but he was imprisoned by the Spanish

Inquisition for a year and a half. Finally in
1566 Buchanan was appointed Principal
of St Leonard's College at the University
of St Andrews and later became tutor to
King James VI.

Return again to the path on your left
past the large holly bush. The magnificent
tomb of Elizabeth Paton faces you, framed
by two semi-clothed men, by four corinthian columns, the screaming head of a
monster and the seated crowned figure of
Death. Four winged souls look out below.

Return to the path. As you do so you
will notice under the tree the simple slabstone of [27] Captain **JOHN PORTEOUS**
(*d* 1736). Jock Porteous was the son of a
Canongate tailor and trained as a tailor,
but he was so difficult to handle that his
father packed him off to the army where
he served in Holland with the Scots Dutch
Brigade.

He returned to Edinburgh as drill-
master of the Town Guard around 1715.
Three years later he was an Ensign with
the Guard which at that time consisted of
100 men in three companies. Porteous was
made a captain in 1726 with 30 men
under his command.

Ten years later a smuggler, the dyer
Andrew Wilson, was sentenced to be
hanged. He was taken to the Grassmarket
at the foot of the West Bow where the

CAPTAINS of the TOWN GUARD (*after* KAY)

gallows stood in a block of sandstone. The
black-masked executioner held the rope,
the town drummer beat out a roll and
Wilson was hoisted up. The magistrate
went for the customary 'deid-chack'
(execution meal) to a neighbouring tavern
and half an hour later waved a white rod
out of the window as a signal for Wilson's
body to be cut down.

As the hangman stepped forward to do
this he was stoned by the crowd, one of
whom cut the rope. At the same time a
hail of stones and earth was flung at the
Town Guard and their Captain.

In the confusion he ordered the Guard
to fire. Three civilians were killed and
twelve wounded. In a fury the mob chased
the Guard up the West Bow and in a panic
the Guard fired again, killing three more.

Porteous was put on trial, found guilty,
but reprieved (for political reasons) by the

Regent, Queen Caroline. Immediately
what were to become known as the
Porteous Riots broke out all over the city.
The mob stole the keys of the West Port
and locked all the town gates.

Then they broke into the Guard House
in the middle of the High Street, seized
guns, Lochaber axes and the town drum,
tried to set fire to the Tolbooth (where
Porteous was being held) and managed to
break in and drag him into the street where
they lynched him on a dyer's pole, after
burning his feet.

'*All passion spent*' reads the modern
headstone—both that of Porteous and that
of the mob.

Continue down the path. Take the
steps down. As you reach the bottom step,
look left at the small iron grill leading
into a tomb under the grass. It seems to
lead into an underground world, a secret
city of the dead. There are several skull
and cross-bone plaques set into the wall.
This is the last resting-place of the Spanish
portrait painter [28] **JOHN MEDINA**
(1659-1710), knighted by Queen Anne in
1707—the last knight created in Scotland
before the Union.

Walk down over the grass along the
wall of the burial ground. Here you see a
sequence of highly ornate memorials, black
and beige carvings filled with dramatic

life—angels playing musical instruments, cherubs, skulls, headless figures of Justice and Mercy, twisted and deformed pillars —all full of noise and movement.

In front of the tomb of **[29] THOMAS BANNATYNE** (1570-1635), a wealthy merchant, a large carved slab is imbedded in the ground. Originally this was fixed to the top of the tomb but it fell down.

On it a large fat baby sits in front of Holyrood Palace. In spite of his wealth, Bannatyne must have been a melancholy man—the observation on his tomb reads: *'What is life? A shadow, a smoke, a flower'*.

At the bottom of the wall turn right towards the two walled graves. As you approach the first you see a cylindrical stone stump jutting right out of the ground with the initials 'J. E. M.' This is the grave of the fourth Earl of Morton, **[30] JAMES DOUGLAS** (*c* 1516-81); and the stone is a copy of the original wooden log driven into the ground to mark burials at the time.

Regent of Scotland from 1572-78, the Earl was a keen supporter of the Reformation and the alliance with England. He was dismissed for having taken part in the murder of David Rizzio, the Italian secretary to Mary Queen of Scots, and it was also known that he had advance warning of the plot to kill

Henry Lord Darnley (Mary's husband).

Having brought over the 'Maiden' from the Continent in 1564 (Edinburgh's early version of the guillotine), it is ironic that it was that dreadful instrument which sliced off his head.

His body was taken down from the place of execution and carried to the Tolbooth. Then it was buried secretly at night in Greyfriars. His head was impaled on the spikes fixed to the Netherbow Port. Eighteen months later, by order of King James VI, the Earl of Morton's head was reunited with his body.

The 'MAIDEN'

Walk on to the tablestone with the small tilted stone below. [31] **Dr ARCH-IBALD PITCAIRNE** (1652-1713) rests under it, a founder of the Royal College of Physicians, Professor of Physic at Leyden in Holland, a keen Jacobite, poet and wit. Although a founder member of the College of Physicians, he practised anatomy, annually dissecting a human body provided by the Town Council. In 1701 Pitcairne became a fellow of the Royal College of Surgeons.

He was said to have been an atheist, mainly because he was sharply critical of the puritanical ways of some Kirk members and he did not hide the fact.

Pitcairne liked his wine and he used to send his servant out after dark to bring more bottles to the house. He was said to have been 'drunk twice every day'.

An ardent, but secret, Jacobite, Pitcairne ordered several bottles of wine to be buried with him with the proviso that they were to be drunk only when a Stuart came to the throne of Scotland. However, when his gravestone was being restored, the bottles had mysteriously disappeared.

Go on four paces—at your feet now lies **[32] JAMES CRAIG** (1744-95), who at 23 years of age won the competition to design Edinburgh's New Town.

Craig (whose instruments and plans can be seen in Huntly House Museum) also designed the once-fashionable Merchant Street under George IV Bridge, the Gothic Observatory on Calton Hill built for the astronomer Thomas Short and the entrance to Leith Fort.

The quotation on the stone is from his uncle, the poet James Thomson's 'Prospect of Great Britain':

August, around, what public works I see!
Lo! Stately streets, Lo! Squares that court
    the breeze,
Even fram'd with elegance the plain retreat,
The private dwelling. Certain in his aim,
Taste, never idly working, saves expence.

Now turn half right towards the large obelisk eight paces away. Far off, from the Highlands, you can almost hear the bagpipes calling on the wind. The monument is decorated with a basket-hilted claymore, a targe (shield), shepherd's crook, hunting-horn, scrolls of poems, a rifle, a partridge, an antlered deer, a rabbit and a pistol. This monument commemorates the great Highland poet and soldier [33] **DUNCAN BAN MACINTYRE** (1724-1812).

Macintyre was a soldier with the Breadalbane Fencibles who fought against the Jacobites at the Battle of Falkirk Muir in 1746.

Shortly afterwards the Fencibles were disbanded and Macintyre worked as a forester and gamekeeper for 20 years until unfairly dismissed. He had no choice but to leave his family and glen and come down to the city of Edinburgh where he joined the Town Guard.

With his wife he manufactured and sold illicit whisky in a Lawnmarket 'howff'. Although he never learned to read, he became one of the major Gaelic poets and travelled through the Highlands, wearing Highland dress, selling his works. On his head was a checked bonnet from which hung the large bushy tail of a wild animal. A badger's skin was fastened by a belt in front of him, a sword was at his side and a soldier's wallet strapped across his broad shoulders.

Next walk left towards the green hedge and wooden bench. Go round the side of the hedge to the left, to the tall monument at the wall above Candlemaker Row—the **[34] MARTYRS MONUMENT** with its triangular pediment on top and ionic columns and large scrolls on each side framing the text of a long prayer to those who died for the cause.

Greyfriars Kirk has an important place in the history of the National Covenant. The Covenant was a protest by Scottish

The MARTYRS MONUMENT

Presbyterians against the new English forms of worship introduced by Charles I. The first copy of the document was drawn up in the Taylors' Hall in the Cowgate and then brought up to Greyfriars on 28 February 1638 to be signed by nobles and lairds, before being taken back to the Cowgate to be signed by ministers and representatives of the towns.

In June 1679 at Bothwell Bridge the Covenanters were finally defeated. Twelve hundred of them were roped in pairs and taken to Edinburgh where they were held in Greyfriars churchyard (then a grass park of some three acres surrounded by high walls), the wounded being cared for in Heriot's Hospital close by. Here for five months the Covenanters lived in the open with no shelter and little food.

Within two weeks 400 of them were sentenced to be transported to the Plantations in the West Indies and many were released after promising not to rebel again. In early August one Covenanter, John Kid, was tortured by the 'boots' which crushed his legs. He and another Covenanter were then publicly executed. Only 340 prisoners were left by November. Five were hanged in chains and 250 sent by sea to the West Indies. Off Orkney the ship sank in a storm—most were drowned, trapped below the decks.

The Martyrs Monument (a copy—the original is in Huntly House Museum in the Canongate) records that: 'From May 27th 1661, when the most noble Marquis of Argyle was beheaded, to the 17th of February 1688 when Mr Renwick suffered, were one way or other Murdered and Destroyed for the same Cause, about Eighteen thousand, of whom were executed at Edinburgh almost a hundred of Noblemen, Gentlemen, Ministers and Others, noble Martyrs for Jesus Christ. The most of them lie here'. Under the inscription flowers grow in the bed through most of the year.

To the west of the monument, in a long trench, more than 100 Covenanters were buried.

Turn back towards the church and walk to the middle of the retaining wall, below the large expanse of grass bordering the church. Above the terrace, in an unmarked grave, lies [35] **WILLIAM RITCHIE** (1781-1831), solicitor and founder in 1817, with his friend Charles Maclaren, of *The Scotsman* newspaper.

In the middle of the terrace wall a large urn, almost an Aladdin's lamp, stands below an inscription dedicated to [36] **HENRY MACKENZIE** (1745-1831). Mackenzie was an Edinburgh solicitor who became Attorney for the Crown in Scotland. He was best known as a writer of essays, plays and novels and nicknamed 'The Man of Feeling' from the title of his popular novel of that name published in 1771, a book which wallowed in excessive 'tear-jerking'.

Turn left and walk over to the cobbled path. Go right at the black street-lamp. When you reach the cherry trees, go left across the grass towards Candlemaker Row.

Surrounded by pink gravel and pink cobbles is the pink and grey stone of {37} **JOHN GRAY** (1813-58), standing close beside the old tablestone under which his wee dog sheltered for so many years.

John Gray—'Auld Jock'—a police constable, lived in the Cowgate with his trained police dog, Bobby. PC Gray saw to the safety of the livestock at the weekly market in the Grassmarket. In 1857 he contracted tuberculosis and died the following year. His faithful Skye terrier, {38} **'GREYFRIARS BOBBY'**, accompanied the funeral procession and stayed at his master's graveside for 14 years.

As you leave the churchyard, stop beside the pink granite headstone at the entrance erected by the Dog Aid Society in 1981.

Just outside the entrance to Greyfriars Kirk once stood John Traill's Refreshment Rooms where Bobby was fed for his 14 long years of watching and waiting at his master's grave.

In 1867, Bobby, legally a stray dog and liable to be put down, was licensed by Edinburgh's Lord Provost in recognition of his extraordinary faithfulness. His statue by William Brodie, was later erected by Baroness Burdett-Coutts opposite the churchyard entrance, a drinking-fountain below it to quench the thirst of weary travellers.

Greyfriars Bobby's dish, collar and the cup from the drinking-fountain (shut off in 1957) are in the Huntly House Museum.

Now take a seat on one of the nearby benches in the churchyard, breathe deeply and close your eyes. Focus your thoughts on a number of other great names buried here in unmarked graves: people like the unfortunate Bailie **JOHN MACMORRAN** who was shot and killed trying to sort out a sit-in by the boys of the High School in 1595 as they protested over the reduction in their Autumn holiday. Or the first Principal of Edinburgh University **ROBERT ROLLOCK**. Or the 'Van Dyck of Scotland', the famous portrait painter **GEORGE JAMESON**.

And what about the inimitable **WILLIAM McGONAGALL** (1825-1902), prince of clowns, the 'world's worst poet', who was born and who died in the Cowgate? In November 1895 he performed his poem 'The Battle of Bannockburn' to the fun-loving Junior Section of the Leith Liberal Club, waving his stick wildly as he proclaimed, *'The Englishmen from the Scots did fly, And left many thousands on the field quite dead to die ...'*

Have a quiet giggle at his amiable nonsense and then open your eyes.

TOMBS in GREYFRIARS CHURCHYARD

N

PARLIAMENT SQUARE

HIGH STREET

6

1
2

3
5 4

7

ST GILES CATHEDRAL

ST GILES

Enter through the main western door under the intricate patterns of stone crowding on stone. On the wind you may hear the distant voices which once worshipped in the ancient kirk.

Turn left into the church. Inside all is still and dark—a place of peace now. Pass the garlanded kneeling angel on your left, even though she offers you a white marble scallop shell.

Up in the mysterious shadows of the roof, stone locks on rugged stone. The second chapel you come to on the left, past the dark bronze figure of John Knox, holds the tomb of cross-eyed Archibald Campbell ('Gillespie Gruamach'), the [1] **MARQUESS** of **ARGYLL** (1607-61), clutching a sword with a basket-hilt, his head on a cushion, his right hand on the Bible (with a sprig of heather beside it), his feet crossed in elegant shoes.

Argyll was a devout Presbyterian, controlling his enormous estates from Inverary Castle. As chief of the Clan Campbell, he had 5000 men at his

The
SEAL of
ST GILES

disposal. When Charles I came to Scotland in 1641 to make peace with the Covenanters, he created Campbell, their leader, the first Marquess of Argyll.

Seven years later the most fervent Covenanters marched on Edinburgh, swept the Government aside and left Argyll in almost complete control—he was thus able to allow Oliver Cromwell into Edinburgh with a warm welcome from the citizens.

After Charles I was executed the captured Earl of Montrose was imprisoned in Edinburgh, tortured and taken up the High Street under the scornful eyes of Argyll himself, watching from Moray House. Montrose was hanged at the Mercat Cross; his limbs hacked off and his head stuck on the Tolbooth roof as a terrible warning.

In 1651 it was Argyll who crowned Charles II at Scone, placing the crown on the king's head. But his luck was about to turn—only ten years after Montrose's dismembered body was given a hero's burial in Edinburgh, Argyll was taken prisoner in Edinburgh Castle, executed in the High Street, his head impaled on the Tolbooth.

As you leave the tomb, look at the first pillar on your left. There a brass inscription framed in red polished marble commemorates [2] James Dalrymple, **VISCOUNT**

STAIR (1619-95), Professor of Philosophy by the age of 23. He gave up academic life and became an advocate in 1648. He was made a judge by Oliver Cromwell in 1657 and this appointment was also allowed to stand by Charles II at the Restoration.

He became Lord President of the Court of Session in 1670 and two years later MP for Wigtown.

Having fought for the Covenanters as a young man, Lord Stair did not approve of the harsh treatment which the Covenanters were later given. His wife was taken into custody for attending Covenanter meetings and Lord Stair was charged with complicity.

He escaped to Holland in 1682 and was charged with treason for being involved in the 1679 Rebellion and the Rye House Plot, but returned with William of Orange in 1688 and was reinstated as Lord President.

He was best known for his monumental work on the Scottish legal system—*The Institutions of the Law of Scotland* (1681)—which laid down the basis of legal practice in Scotland, making it a coherent system.

The mysterious disappearance of his daughter Janet in 1669, only a month after her wedding, inspired Walter Scott's novel *The Bride of Lammermuir*, and Donizetti's opera of the same name.

Now cross to the opposite side of the

church in the direction of Parliament
House (south).

On the left hand side of the mighty
organ is the Chepman Aisle, the resting-
place of [3] **WALTER CHEPMAN** (1473-
1538), an Edinburgh merchant and Clerk
in the office of the King's Secretary (1494).
He financed the first Scottish commercial
printing press under the direction of the
master printer Andrew Myllar.

Myllar trained as a printer at Rouen
in France where he had two books
published. He set up as a bookseller in
Edinburgh, and in 1507 he and Chepman
were given the Royal Patent to acquire a
printing press with all the tools and
equipment necessary and the craftsmen to
operate it.

Myllar's craftsmen and the Gothic
typefaces were French. It is this which
makes the earliest Scottish printed books
different from those printed in England
by William Caxton (who was German-
trained). The press of Chepman and
Myllar in the Cowgate was in full
operation between 1508 and 1510. All
that remains today of their printed books
are some poetic tales, parts of the poem
'The Wallace' and the famous Aberdeen
Breviary (clerical prayerbook).

Chepman used his wealth in 1513 to
found a chapel dedicated to the memory of

his patron James IV of Scotland and was himself buried there.

Opposite Chepman is the tomb of {4} John Graham, 3rd **EARL of MONTROSE** (1547-1608) who fought at the Battle of Langside on Regent Moray's side. James VI thought highly of him and in 1584 he was appointed a Lord of Session (judge). He had been chancellor of the jury at the trial of Regent Morton, 1581.

When James VI became King of England (and moved to London), Montrose was one of those put in charge of Scotland —as Viceroy.

In the same tomb is his grandson James Graham, {5} 1st **MARQUESS of MONTROSE** (1612-50), a romantic man of action. Now you see him lying on his tomb, holding a fresh bunch of white heather bound with tartan ribbon. Beside him is a copy of the National Covenant— he was one of the first to sign—which inspired him to perform incredible feats of soldiering under the skilled guidance of Colkitto (Alastair MacDonald).

Montrose worked hard to make Charles I accept the Covenant. Then Montrose changed sides, opposing the Covenanters. Charles made him Lieutenant-General in Scotland and Montrose began a series of masterly victories. At Tippermuir he defeated the Covenanters, captured Aberdeen and started off on unexpected marches through the Highlands. He surprised the Marquess of Argyll in his own castle of Inverary and then again at Inverlochy in the middle of winter.

After going into exile on the Continent, Montrose returned to Scotland in 1650, marching down from Orkney. However, on this occasion he was finally defeated and taken prisoner.

When Montrose arrived in Edinburgh he had already been declared a traitor. He was met by the town officials, his hands tied and he was fastened to a seat in the executioner's wagon. In this degrading position he was taken up the Royal Mile, past Moray House (where the Marquess of Argyll left a wedding reception to watch Montrose as he passed).

Montrose wrote his own epitaph:

Let them bestow on ev'ry Airth a Limb;
Open all my Veins, that I may swim
To Thee my Saviour, in that Crimson Lake;
Then place my purboiled Head upon a Stake;
Scatter my Ashes, throw them in the Air:
Lord (since Thou know'st where all these
*   Atoms are)*
I'm hopeful, once Thou'lt recollect my Dust,
And confident Thou'lt raise me with the Just.

He proved to be an accurate prophet of his own fate. In 1661 the many parts of his dismembered body were reunited and buried with due pomp and ceremony.

Go past the organ. In the next aisle is the austere grey monument to [6] the **EARL of MORAY** (1531-70), James Stewart: the illegitimate son of James V (and so the half brother of Mary Queen of Scots).

He was a statesman with a broad vision and deep understanding of political events. Although he supported the Reformers, he also allowed Queen Mary to worship in the Catholic manner in her private chapel. But he saw to it that the future James VI received a Protestant education and understood the ways of the English, so that when the time came he could be king of both Scotland and England.

Moray was a key figure in the government of Scotland up to the point in 1565 when Mary decided to marry Darnley. Moray supported Darnley's resentment of the growing power of Mary's well-bred Italian secretary, the suave David Riccio with the dark, seductive singing voice.

Later, when Mary married Bothwell, the Earl of Moray was safe in England giving evidence against his half-sister. And after the Queen abdicated, he became Regent for the young king James.

In January 1570 Regent Moray was travelling from Stirling to Edinburgh when he was shot dead by Hamilton of

Bothwellhaugh (whose life, ironically, he had saved at the Battle of Langside two years earlier).

John Knox preached at Moray's funeral and an inscription by the poet George Buchanan was fixed into the monument.

Leave the church the way you came. In Parliament Square, turn left and make for the lead statue of Charles II on horseback. Now you may hear a powerful voice echoing round the porticoes of the High Court. For, not far from the statue of the Merry Monarch, in parking lot No 44, is the grave of [7] **JOHN KNOX** (1512-72). Knox, buried in St Giles churchyard some years after it was declared closed, was the figurehead of the Reformation in Scotland. Trained as a Catholic priest and Papal notary (solicitor), he was an expert in Canon Law. His skill in public speaking was sharpened by his legal training and his bitter experiences of life in slavery.

Knox was born near Haddington, East Lothian. The executions of Scottish Reformers like Patrick Hamilton (1528) and George Wishart (1546) hardened his conviction that the Church in Scotland badly needed to be reformed. To help him in this mammoth task, he turned first to England for support.

Following the assassination of Cardinal David Beaton at St Andrews in 1546,

Knox returned to Scotland to help the Reformed community as a Protestant minister. However, St Andrews was captured by the French and Knox was made a galley-slave for two years until King Edward VI of England secured his release.

In England, Knox was a minister at Newcastle, Berwick and in London before being appointed Royal Chaplain. He advised Archbishop Cranmer on the drawing up of the new *Articles of Religion,* contributed to the writing of the *Second Prayer Book* and later composed his own *History of the Reformation in Scotland* (1587).

During the reign of the Catholic Queen Mary, Knox was in Frankfurt and Geneva, absorbing the Reformed theology of John Calvin. He returned once more to Scotland in 1559, becoming minister of St Giles. In his *Book of Discipline* (1560 and 1568) he set out a far-reaching plan for a Church with no bishops, a programme of universal comprehensive education and a nation-wide system of poor relief.

Knox was a powerful opponent against the French ways of Mary Queen of Scots, with a hypnotic gift for denunciation and prophetic criticism. In 1572 he came back to Scotland and preached in St Giles for the last time, being so weak he had to be supported by his friends.

GRAVE of JOHN KNOX

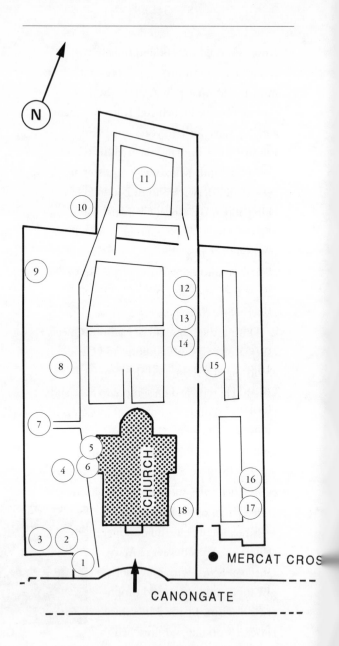

CANONGATE CHURCHYARD

4

CANONGATE

The first thing that strikes you about the
Canongate Kirk is the golden skull and
antlers of a deer high on the roof above the
pillared porch. This commemorates the
legendary escape of King David I from a
wild stag in the Forest of Drumsheugh and
his dazzling vision of the Cross between
its antlers. It is the traditional symbol of
the Canongate.

For centuries Holyrood Abbey was the
parish church for the Canongate but in
1686 King James VII decided to turn the
Abbey church into a Chapel Royal for the
Order of the Thistle and made the parish-
ioners leave. In 1691 the Canongate Kirk
was opened as a replacement.

Go through the main gate under a
canopy of ornamental cherry trees and turn
first left. Set into a wall of the Canongate
Tolbooth which faces you, overlooking a
small plot of lush grass framed by railings,
is the slabstone commemorating [1] Lord
Provost **GEORGE DRUMMOND** (1687-
1766) whose true monument is Edinburgh's
New Town.

Drummond was Edinburgh's greatest
Lord Provost (he served six terms from

1725 to 1764), the driving force behind the building of the New Town, and a founder of the Royal Infirmary in 1738, the North Bridge in 1763. He also backed the construction of the City Chambers (then known as the Royal Exchange), the elegant St Cecilia's concert hall in the Cowgate and the draining of the Nor' Loch which formed Princes Street Gardens.

GEORGE DRUMMOND

Drummond was a tall Perthshire lad with a clear head for figures. By the age of 20 he had become Accountant General of Excise. He rose rapidly through the ranks of the Edinburgh Town Council, took part in the General Assembly of the Church of Scotland and played an influential role in the appointment of many of the finest professors at the University of Edinburgh (which was under the control of the Town Council).

He was also a soldier, having fought for the Hanoverians at the Battle of Sherrifmuir in 1715. When the Jacobites attacked Edinburgh 30 years later, he was in command of the 1st (College) Company. Unfortunately his men turned out to be too timid to fight and ran away!

Drummond married four times and had 14 children. His diary, written in 1738, shows him continually dogged by debt and self-doubt: 'I am now entered my fifty-second year and alas how little progress have I made on my way to heaven'.

Go left again to the rear of the Tolbooth to the burial ground of the economist [2] **ADAM SMITH** (1723-90), framed by high black railings, topped by graceful French *fleur-de-lys*.

The handsome but austere monument set against the wall is topped by an urn; a bearded classical head stares from the centre of an arch of radiating ridges like rays of light, and a small medallion hangs from a ribbon with simple swathes of cloth falling away at each side.

Smith, born in Kirkcaldy, Fife, is best known as a pioneer of modern Economics. His book *Wealth of Nations* (1776) had an immediate impact on politicians and a lasting influence on businessmen. Smith showed how the division of labour could improve productivity and also how value comes from the labour used in production. He taught that in a market economy the profit motive could be made to work for the good of the whole community.

He was educated at the universities of Glasgow and Oxford, lecturing first in English Literature at Edinburgh. Then he became Professor of Moral Philosophy at Glasgow. In later years he was tutor to the

Duke of Buccleuch, receiving a pension for life.

He ended his days as a Commissioner for Customs and then settled into a comfortable lifestyle at nearby Panmure House in the Canongate until his death.

One of Smith's most likeable sides was his continual absentmindedness—this led him into some hilarious situations. While Professor of Moral Philosophy in Glasgow he took a friend to see a well-known tannery. The two of them were standing on a plank laid over the tanning-pit, Smith talking excitedly about his favourite topic —the division of labour. He completely forgot where he was, stepped to one side and fell head first into the dye-bath. He was pulled out straight away, stripped, wrapped in blankets and carried home in a sedan chair where he complained that he was about to die from the cold!

Next to the grave of Adam Smith is the grey granite sarcophagus of Aberdonian {3} **JAMES GREGORY** (1753-1821) and other members of his family. Gregory's lasting claim to fame is not so much in his professorship of Medicine at Edinburgh, or being the leading consultant in Scotland, but in his marvellous brown 'Gregory's Mixture' made from magnesia, rhubarb and ginger, which brought relief to upset stomachs for many generations.

Now turn towards the classical façade
of the former Royal High School far above
you on the slopes of Calton Hill. Walk
towards the far end of the church where
you see the single round window. Just
before you get there, look to your left at
the tall Greek obelisk to the generous
plumber {4} **GEORGE CHALMERS**
(1773-1836). When he died, he left the
sum of £30,000 towards the construction
of Chalmers Hospital in Lauriston Place.
The elegance of his monument matches
his generosity.

From the Chalmers obelisk, continue
directly to the church. Under the round
window is the memorial to two artist
brothers—{5} **ALEXANDER RUNCI-
MAN** (1736-85) bare-headed; and {6}
JOHN RUNCIMAN (1744-68) with the
natty hat, coat and fancy lace at his neck.

Having studied the works of Raphael
and Michaelangelo in Italy, Alexander
painted a number of murals in Scotland.
One of these can be seen on the ceiling of
the nearby St Patrick's Church in the Cowgate. Alexander was a sociable but fiery-
tempered man. He eventually dropped
dead in West Nicholson Street, partly as a
result of physical stress from lying on his
back while painting ceilings. His brother
John was a promising painter, but died
tragically young on a visit to Naples.

Continue down the path in the direction of Calton Hill. As you reach the end of the church, turn hard left up a path of pink granite chips. Walk eleven paces to the simple grey slabstone with its plot of roses fenced off by heavy chainlinks. This is the grave of the young poet [7] **ROBERT FERGUSSON** (1750-74), who died in tragic circumstances.

Fergusson worked as a humble legal clerk in spite of having a university degree and he wrote songs which he would perform at private houses in Edinburgh. His demise was tragic—sudden changes of mood and a hint of mental instability produced by a serious fall down a flight of steps, led to him being committed to the Bedlam (Insane Asylum). There he took his own life and was buried in a pauper's grave.

Fergusson, whom Robert Burns greatly admired, wrote with a fresh and colourful eye, full of humour and observation. One of his best poems—'Auld Reekie'—is a celebration of the sights and sounds of street life in Scotland's capital:

> *Now Morn, with bonny purple smiles,*
> *Kisses the air-cock o' Saunt Giles;*
> *Rakin their een, the servant lasses*
> *Early begin their lies and clashes.*
> *On stair, wi' tub or pat in hand,*
> *The barefoot housmaids loe to stand,*

That antrin folk may ken how snell
Auld Reekie will at mornin smell.

While in the Bedlam he suffered from delusions, imagining himself to be a king, putting a crown of pleated straw on his head. After two months he died in his cell on his bed of straw, in the terrors of the night, amid the howls of insanity. There was no one to help or pity him.

FERGUSSON'S
GRAVE

When Burns came to Edinburgh in 1787 he was so angry at the absence of a memorial to Fergusson that he asked permission from the Town Council to pay for a stone and epitaph. Burns' words on the stone read:

No sculptured marble here, nor pompous lay,
No storied Urn, nor animated Bust;
This simple Stone directs Pale Scotia's way
To pour her Sorrows o'er her poet's Dust.

Now walk down over the grass towards Nelson's Monument high above. At about 26 paces is the slabstone dedicated in 1766 to the [8] **SOCIETY of COACH-DRIVERS,** whose members are buried anonymously around the stone. On the top

is a skull gnawing a thigh-bone—a
reminder that Death is never far away
(especially on the roads!) Below, a coach
and four rattles over the first North Bridge
(built only three years previously), the
coach-driver cracking his whip.

Walk diagonally down towards the end
of the boundary wall on your left. The
third last memorial on the wall (head-high
below three coping-stones) is of the Revd
Alexander Brunton and his wife, novelist
[9] **MARY BRUNTON** (1778-1818).

Mary Brunton was born in Orkney. She
was a good musician and spoke French
and Italian. At the age of 19 she eloped
with a young minister. Much of her adult
life was spent as a country minister's wife
in East Lothian, but when her husband
moved to Edinburgh as minister of Greyfriars Kirk, she wrote her first novel, *Self-
Control* (1811), enlivened with exciting
adventures sugaring a moral message. Then
she wrote a second, *Discipline* (1815).

She had begun a third novel when she
died giving birth to her first baby (still-
born).

Turn right and go to the path, walking
towards the slim white Gothic steeple
monument. At the path, turn left to the
great mass of ivy covering the black and
beige stones of the tomb built for [10]
DUGALD STEWART (1753-1828),

Professor of Moral Philosophy.

Stewart was a magnetic lecturer with a national reputation. In his house in the Canongate he took young students as lodgers: one of them was the future Prime Minister, Lord Palmerston. In his early days as a lecturer he would get up at 3 o' clock in the morning and prepare his lectures while walking in the garden.

Now look up. On the brow of Calton Hill, high above Dugald Stewart's tomb, is the Greek temple designed in his honour by W H Playfair, and erected in 1832.

Standing alone in the centre of the grassy enclosure is a very tall polished granite pillar decorated at the bottom by crossed muskets with fixed bayonets and a soldier's ammunition belt. It was erected by the proprietor of the nearby Holyrood Glassworks, William Ford, in May 1880.

This commemorates the many {11} **SOLDIERS** who died while on garrison duty at Edinburgh Castle between 1692 and 1880 and who are buried around the pillar, the Castle being part of the Canongate parish. The monument was paid for by William Ford of the local glassworks.

If you close your eyes perhaps you can hear the sounds of battle, the trumpets, the wail of the bagpipes, the thunder of cannon and the screams of dying men.

Now walk back to the church along

the other boundary through the doorway in the wall. You hear a different sound— the jovial echo of an eighteenth century bassoon running up and down the scale, the tuning-up of a theatre orchestra. Continue up the path towards the largest enclosed grave on your left. Three graves before you reach it is the honey-coloured but badly damaged memorial wall-stone to {12} **JOHANN FREDERICK LAMPE** (1703-51), a German musician and composer, said to have been Handel's favourite bassoon-player in London. Lampe is thought to have played the contra-bassoon at the coronation of George I.

At the Edinburgh pleasure gardens, Lampe introduced the London fashion of open-air concerts—a fashion which still continues today in Princes Street Gardens.

He also composed around 13 operas and three pantomimes and wrote a book on musical theory—*A plain and compendious method of Teaching Thorough-Bass* (1737). An extract from this work can be seen at the top of his monument, the pages held open by two winged cherubs.

Proceed now to the impressive mausoleum of {13} Sir **WILLIAM FETTES** (1750-1836), tea and wine merchant, Lord Provost and founder of Fettes College on his estate of Comely Bank.

Look down at the small brass plaque

on the left front of the monument. It records the burial nearby of [14] **JAMES BALLANTYNE** (1772-1833), a Kelso solicitor turned printer and publisher who printed Sir Walter Scott's *The Minstrelsy of the Scottish Border* and his novels. Ballantyne lived in St John Street in the Canongate and his printing business was just below the Calton Hill. He was a generous, sociable character. In fact, on the day of Ballantyne's funeral, standing at the graveside of his friend, Scott whispered, 'I feel as if there would be less sunshine for me from this day forth'.

Walk on again up the slope and turn first left between two gate-pillars, into the other section of the churchyard. Directly to your left is the stately monument marked 'Earnock and Dalnair', with the bronze profile of the landscape painter [15] **HUGH 'Greek' WILLIAMS** (1773-1829) set into the pink granite.

Williams was born on his father's ship during a voyage to the West Indies. He was orphaned early and brought up in Edinburgh by a grandmother who had married a cultured Italian. He encouraged Williams to draw and paint. Success in painting Highland landscapes was followed by a tour to Italy and Greece. This led to an outpouring of watercolours. Lord Cockburn wrote that he was 'by far the

finest painter in water-colours that Scotland
has yet produced'.

Walk forward to the boundary wall
and turn right. Now you hear a new kind
of music—a sad Scots song sung by an
Ayrshire lad. The third plot on the left is
the burial ground of {16} WILLIAM,
Lord CRAIG (1745-1813), Senator of the
College of Justice; and his cousin {17}
AGNES MACLEHOSE (Nancy Craig)
(1759-1841). Her delightful profile is to
be seen on a golden plaque, just as it
might have charmed her friend Robert
Burns (a relationship of which Lord Craig
certainly disapproved). She wears a low-
cut gown, a scarf twisted through her hair.

Nancy Craig was the beautiful and
intelligent daughter of a Glasgow surgeon.
When only 17, she married a lawyer. The
marriage was not a happy one and after
four years they went their separate ways.

After her father's death, she and her
children went to Edinburgh to stay with
her cousin Lord Craig in York Place.

In December 1787 Nancy Craig met
Robert Burns at Miss Nimmo's house in
Alison Square and invited him to her
house in Potterrow for tea. The day before
they were due to meet again, Burns
injured his leg and had to stay in his room
for six weeks. During this time they wrote
letters to each other which (in the case of

Burns at least) burned with passion.

Later they met more often and in 1791 for the last time. Burns wrote for her one of his finest songs:

> *Ae fond kiss, and then we sever;*
> *Ae farewell, and then for ever!*
> *Deep in heart-wrung tears I'll pledge thee,*
> *Warring sighs and groans I'll wage thee.*

Walk forward, turn right towards the church and then glance left as you go, to the old Canongate Burgh Cross, central meeting-place of the people of the Canongate, for gossip and trade.

CANONGATE
MARKET
CROSS

Walk to the wall of the church and you hear a strong dark foreign voice singing a folksong of Italy. Between the first and second window is the uneven flatstone grave of the Italian secretary and musician to Mary Queen of Scots, **{18} DAVID RICCIO/RIZZIO** (*c* 1533-66).

Born in Turin, Riccio was the son of a musician. He first came to Scotland in 1561 as secretary to the Marquis of Moreto. When Mary Queen of Scots told Moreto that she needed a bass singer for her chapel choir, he recommended Riccio. Shortly afterwards he was made Mary's secretary.

Wanting to avoid her weak husband, Henry Lord Darnley, and caught between her Scots and French subjects, the Queen began to confide increasingly in Riccio—a relationship which caused much talk and envy.

On 9 March 1566 the Queen was dining at Holyrood with Riccio and a few close friends when Darnley came into the room, followed by a group of armed men. They seized Riccio, took him to another room and stabbed him 56 times. His body was then thrown out into the courtyard below.

Tradition has it that at the time of the Rebellion (1688) Riccio's body was taken from Holyrood and re-buried in the churchyard of the Canongate.

CANONGATE CHURCH

5

HOLYROOD ABBEY

Walking into the ruins of the Abbey church is an experience both moving and horrific. The great Methodist preacher John Wesley records in 1780: 'The roof of the royal chapel is fallen in and the bones of James V and the once beautiful Lord Darnley are scattered about like those of sheep'.

Hugo Arnot, 19 years later, recalls the Revolution at the time of James VII, when the mob 'broke into the vault which had been used as the royal sepulchre in which lay the bodies of King James V, of Madeleine of France, his first Queen and of the Earl of Darnley and others of the monarchs and royal family of Scotland.

'They broke open the lead coffins, carried off the lids but left the rest. When we lately visited it, upon looking into the vaults, the doors of which were open, we found that what had escaped the fury of the mob at the revolution became a prey to the rapacity of the mob who ransacked the church after it fell in December 1768. In 1776 we had seen the body of James V and some others in their lead coffins. Now the coffins have been stolen.

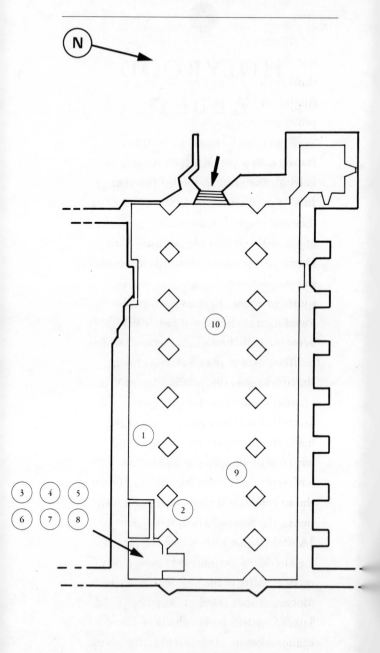

HOLYROOD ABBEY

'The head of Queen Madaleine which was then entire and even beautiful and the skull of Darnley were also stolen. His thigh-bones however still remain and are proofs of the vastness of his stature.'

To a later generation the Chapel was romantic, otherworldly. The composer Felix Mendelssohn, visiting Edinburgh in July 1829, observed that 'The chapel is now roofless, and is overgrown with grass and ivy,' and the ruined altar where Mary Queen of Scots was married. Everything is in ruins and mouldering, and the bright light of Heaven shines in. I believe I have found the beginning of my Scottish Symphony there today'.

In his notebook he had written down the first 16 bars of his Symphony.

Stop at the main entrance to the church. Turn right and walk along between the free-standing pillars and the wall packed with multi-coloured jigsaw stone, until you come to the fifth large pillar. Under the second high window against the wall lies a long thin slab, the grave of [1] Sir **JAMES DOUGLAS** (1560-1608).

The life of Douglas was dominated by revenge. After the beheading of Regent Morton in 1581, Douglas attacked Captain James Stewart who had given evidence against Morton. He killed him, cut off his head and took it away on the end of a spear, leaving his body 'to be devoured by dogs and swine'.

Early on a July morning in 1608, Sir James was walking alone in Edinburgh's High Street when he was in turn attacked by a nephew of Captain Stewart. During the struggle, Douglas was stabbed to death.

Walk on to the second last free-standing pillar and go round it. High on its side, facing the centre of the church, is the stone commemorating [2] Bishop **ADAM BOTHWELL** (1527-93).

Bothwell was a man with a foot in both the religious and secular world. He was born in Edinburgh and was appointed Bishop of Orkney in 1559. Soon after he became a Protestant and in 1563 was made a Lord of Session.

On 15 May 1567, at 4 in the morning, Bishop Bothwell married Mary Queen of Scots to the Earl of Bothwell according to the Reformed ritual (but it was rumoured that he had first married them according to the Roman rite).

After Mary's abdication, Bishop Bothwell crowned and anointed King James VI at Stirling, but by the end of the year the General Assembly called a debate on his conduct as an absentee bishop, an infrequent judge and a suspected Catholic sympathiser.

Bishop Bothwell, clever politician that

he was, talked his way out of a corner. In 1570 he was appointed Bishop of Holyrood and again the Assembly complained that the 27 churches under the control of Holyrood were 'decayit and some made sheepfolds, and some sae ruinous that none dare enter, especially Holyrud Hous'.

In earliest times the remains of all Royalty were buried in front of the High Altar. After the destruction of the monastery in 1544 and 1547 by the English army, only the nave of the church was left standing. The individual Royal tombs were emptied and the remains placed at the south-east corner of the new roofless chapel (around half the size of the original church), within a new Royal Vault, in coffins today covered with purple cloth and studded with gleaming brass rivets shaped like flowers.

Turn to your left and walk towards the end of the church. To your left is the Royal Vault where the remains of the kings and queens of Scotland are buried.

[3] **DAVID II** (1324-71), son of Robert the Bruce and the first king to be buried at Holyrood, was married at the age of five to Joanna (the sister of Edward III of England). Shortly afterwards, Robert the Bruce died and David was crowned at Scone.

The young king never recovered from

being thrust early into the limelight. Edward Balliol, supported by the English, claimed the Scottish throne. He defeated the Scots at Dupplin in 1332 and was crowned king. David and his queen were sent off to France for their own safety for seven long years.

When he was 22 years old, David brought an army to England, fought like a lion but was defeated and captured by the Archbishop of York at Neville's Cross in 1346. He was held prisoner for eleven years until the Scots agreed to pay a ransom of 100,000 merks.

Hardened by experience, David spent the rest of his life rebuilding Edinburgh Castle, constructing the 60 feet high King David's Tower. He also looked for ways of smoothing out relations with the English, but Scots still had heavy taxes to pay south of the Border. David married twice but had no sons and so his nephew, Robert II, succeeded him—the first Stuart king.

[4] **JAMES II** (1430-60), known as 'Fiery Face' due to a red birthmark, was born at Holyrood and became king at the age of six after the murder of his father, James I, in Perth. He was taken by his mother to Edinburgh Castle for safety and there held under house arrest by the Castle Governor until his mother smuggled him out, hidden on the back of a pack-horse.

When only ten James witnessed a
horrific murder in the Castle. His mother
had joined forces with the Governor and
the Regent of Scotland to neutralise the
growing power of the Douglas family. The
18 year old Earl of Douglas was invited to
a banquet at the Castle in 1440. As the
Earl entered, the portcullis dropped, the
gate slammed shut and the Douglas body-
guard was locked out. In the banqueting-
hall the head of a black bull (the symbol
of the Douglas family) was carried into the
table. This was the signal for the Governor's
men to rush in, armed to the teeth. The
young Earl and his brother (in spite of the
protests of the King) were beheaded and
buried inside the Castle.

Finally in 1449, James II took control
of the kingdom , but the Douglases, in
the person of the 8th Earl, continued to
rival the power of the King. James gave
the Earl safe conduct and met him at
Stirling in 1452. He ordered the Earl to
submit to him, but he refused. The King's
men stabbed Douglas to death.

As a ruler James was decisive and
energetic but unpredictable. He built the
first Edinburgh town wall and imported
the giant cannon 'Mons Meg' to the Castle.
At the siege of Roxburgh, James was
standing too close to a cannon. It exploded,
killing him almost instantly.

[5] Queen **MARY of GUELDRES**
(1433-63) was the daughter of the Duke
of Gueldres in Holland. Mary, however,
had spent most of her life at the sophist-
icated court of her flamboyant uncle
Philip of Burgundy. In 1449 he put forward
her name as a possible bride for King
James III of Scotland.

She was only 16 when she landed at
Leith, a charming, attractive girl. Three
hundred Scots soldiers and the Lord Provost of Edinburgh led her to the monastery
of the Greyfriars, set on a small hill
surrounded by ornamental gardens.

A week later she was married in the
Abbey at Holyrood and reigned as Queen
for eleven years. When James was killed at
the siege of Roxburgh, she hurried to the
scene and inspired the Scots to capture the
castle. Then she took her young son quickly
to Kelso and had him crowned king.

During the years when her son was too
young to rule, Mary controlled Scotland
with energetic efficiency; but she died
suddenly in 1463. Behind her she left a
good reputation for religious and social
achievement.

She founded the Collegiate Church of
the Holy Trinity (on the site of the present
Waverley Station) in 1462. This was rebuilt
in 1877 (much altered) at Jeffrey Street.
Next to the Church was Trinity Hospital,

which she also founded to 'house, clothe and feed seven destitute but worthy people'.

Over the centuries this number grew and the Hospital became in time the oldest Edinburgh charity (which still exists). The Hospital building was demolished in 1845.

In the Scottish National Gallery at the Mound is the Holy Trinity altarpiece which gives us a clue as to the magnificence of the original church.

[6] **JAMES V** (1512-42) became King of Scotland when one year old. At first his mother, Margaret Tudor, was Regent, then, when she married the Earl of Angus, it was the Duke of Albany who ruled Scotland in the name of the king.

During these unsettled years the two powerful houses of Hamilton and Douglas fought for control of the country. In 1520, 'Cleanse the Causeway' took place in the Cowgate, where the Douglases with over 500 men fought a merciless running battle with the Hamiltons through the wynds and closes of the High Street. Around 80 Hamiltons died and the Douglases under the Earl of Angus won the day.

In 1524 The Duke of Albany fled to France, James was put in the care of the diplomat Sir David Lindsay (author of *Ane Satyre of the Thrie Estatis*), but Angus took the King prisoner. James, however, escaped from Falkland Palace dressed as a groom and took over the kingdom, asserting his authority, making sure his nobles obeyed him.

James believed strongly in social justice and from time to time would disguise himself in old tattered clothes and go into the homes of the poor to listen to their complaints about how the country was run. For this he was known as 'the Guidman of Ballangeich', the 'Gaberlunzie [beggar] King', the 'King of the Commons'.

After the death of his first wife, Madeleine, James married Mary of Lorraine who, aided by Cardinal Beaton, began to persecute and burn the early Protestant Reformers at the stake. It was finally the execution of George Wishart in 1546 which resulted in widespread disgust in Scotland and the assassination of the hated Cardinal himself.

James V was a gifted poet, in many ways resembling the early promise and brilliance of his uncle, Henry VIII of England. He founded the College of Justice in 1532 and a magnificent window in Parliament House commemorates the occasion. After the defeat of the Scots by Henry VIII, at the battle of Solway Moss, James died of a broken heart.

[7] **MADELEINE of FRANCE** (1520-37) was the daughter of Francis, King of

France (who entertained Henry VIII at the Field of Cloth of Gold in 1520). She married James V of Scotland at Notre Dame Cathedral in Paris in January 1537 in the presence of kings and queens and the nobility of Scotland and France.

At the banquet which followed James gave the guests nuggets of gold mined from the hills of Scotland.

The Royal pair returned to Scotland in May 1537 accompanied by two French warships, bringing with them an enormous collection of jewellery, fine clothes and thoroughbred horses. They landed at Leith.

As she stepped onto Scottish soil Madeleine bent down to kiss the earth, so endearing herself to the whole nation. She received a tremendous welcome and preparations were immediately put in hand for the coronation.

At this point Madeleine, whose health was not strong, took ill. Perhaps the rough Scottish weather was too much for her. Forty days after her landing at Leith she died and was buried in Holyrood Abbey. Five years later James V died and was laid to rest beside his beautiful but tragic queen. They were the last king and queen to be buried in Scotland.

[8] Henry Stewart, **LORD DARNLEY** (1546-67) was born in Yorkshire and was related to the English Royal family

through his mother, Margaret Tudor, sister
of Henry VIII. It was rumoured in 1560
that if Queen Elizabeth of England died,
the Catholics would try to have Darnley
made king. It was then that Darnley was
called for by Queen Elizabeth. He is said
to have played the lute for her. But
although he cut a manly, sporting figure,
he had no real strength of character and
Elizabeth cunningly sent him northwards
to her cousin.

Darnley arrived in Edinburgh in 1564.
He met Mary and danced seductively with

her. Persuaded that an alliance
with Darnley would secure the
English throne for Mary, they
became betrothed. Their
wedding on 29 July was no
love-match but a marriage of political
convenience.

CIPHER of
DARNLEY
and MARY in
EDINBURGH
CASTLE

It was not a successful union. Darnley
drank heavily and was intensely jealous.
Mary's Italian secretary, the charming
singer David Riccio, was murdered in front
of the already pregnant Queen by Darnley
and his accomplices, Darnley's dagger
being left pointedly in the corpse.

Darnley had become an increasing
embarrassment to Mary. He had allowed
himself to be used by the powerful Scottish lords who already resented the foreign-
mannered Queen. He was indiscreet,

betraying confidential state information.

When Darnley caught smallpox he was
sent to the house of Kirk o' Field (on the
site of the present Edinburgh University
Old Quad). In the early morning of 10
February 1567 the house was blown up.
Darnley and his servant were found in
mysterious circumstances in a garden 40
feet away. There were no marks on the
bodies but they seemed to have been
strangled. To this day the true facts of the
matter are not known.

As well as the Royal adults buried in
the Abbey, seven infant princes and three
princesses were laid to rest there between
1430 and 1602.

Let us now leave the Kings and Queens
to rest. For almost 500 years Holyrood
was the burial place of the ordinary people
of the Burgh of Canongate, both inside
the Abbey Church and in the churchyard.
In 1685 James VII closed the churchyard,
but burials in the Chapel Royal continued
into the eighteenth and nineteenth
centuries (for example, that of George Earl
of Caithness in 1889).

Now walk across the church towards
the altar tomb in the centre. It has two
plain shields on the side facing you. This
is the tomb of [9] Sir **JOHN SINCLAIR**
(1754-1835), the editor of the first
Statistical Account of Scotland (1791-98),

compiled from information sent in by
parish ministers from all over Scotland.

He was also Member of Parliament for
Caithness, a member of both the Scottish
and English Bar and founded the British
Wool Society (1791). He became the first
President of the Board of Agriculture and
in 1810 was made a Privy councillor. For
his good works he was knighted and then
set out on a long tour of Europe, later
publishing a description of his travels.

Turn back now to the entrance of the
church by which you came in. Walk
towards the ten white marble ovals set in
stone on the ground. Go to the last one on
the left. This is the grave of [10] **MARIE**,
Duchess of **POMAR** (1830-95).

A high-born Spanish lady living in
Paris, she married first a Spanish count
and then the Earl of Caithness. She called
her house in Paris 'Holyrood' and claimed
she could communicate with Mary Queen
of Scots (whom she idolised and said she
had spoken to during a midnight visit to
the Palace and Abbey). As Countess of
Caithness she had the right to be buried
in the family vault in the Abbey.

As you leave the church, spare a
thought for **JOHN PATERSON**
(1600-63), the location of whose grave is
unknown. He was a shoemaker in the
Canongate, a Canongate Bailie and also an

expert golfer. When the Duke of York (afterwards James VII) was living in Holyrood in 1681, two English nobles claimed that golf was originally an English game. To prove their point they challenged the Duke to a game of golf with a partner of his own choice.

The Duke chose John Paterson because he was the finest golfer in the city and during the game in Leith Links the Englishmen were thrashed. The Duke won a sizeable bet and as a reward for Paterson's help he is said to have given the stake money to Paterson who used it to renovate the family home in the Canongate at what is now knows as 'Golfer's Land'. The shoe-

'A NOTED GOLFER'
(*after* KAY)

maker was also allowed to use a crest showing a right hand gripping a golf club with the motto '*Far and Sure*'.

Last of all, but not least, we come to **DAVID RICCIO/RIZZIO** (1533-66), whose body was thrown out of a Palace window after his murder. The body of the Italian musician and secretary to Mary Queen of Scots was then taken to the porter's lodge and placed on top of a chest. The porter's assistant is said to have

remarked: 'Davie sleepit on this kist
[chest] when he first cam here, an' at the
end he lieth here again—a very ingrate
and misknown knave'.

First the body was buried outside the
south-west door on the left of the present
entrance, so that people coming in and
out of the church would walk over it.
Later, when Mary returned to power, she
had the body removed to the Royal Vault
—but it is believed that it was finally
taken back to the door of the church. Then
it is thought it may have been reinterred
outside the Canongate Kirk where a large
marked stone covers the grave.

WEST FRONT of
HOLYROOD ABBEY CHURCH

OLD CALTON

From the front of the General Post Office
turn right past the sooty, salt-encrusted
alcoves of Waterloo Place, towards the
Nelson Monument high above.

Enter the burial ground through the
black iron gate on your right. The view
that meets you looking up the steps is of
the gigantic pointed [1] **POLITICAL
MARTYRS MONUMENT** silhouetted
against the sky.

Pause for a moment to remember those
men who fought for electoral reform—the
lawyer **THOMAS MUIR** (1765-98); the
farmer **WILLIAM SKIRVING**; barrister
JOSEPH GERRALD; and **THOMAS
PALMER**, a Unitarian minister. **MAUR-
ICE MARGAROT** was the only one of
the five men to return home alive from
Botany Bay in Australia, dying penniless
at the age of 70.

Looking up at the tall black monument
pointing into the wind, you can almost
hear Thomas Muir speaking at the end of
his long trial before the hated Lord Brax-
field: *'When our ashes shall be scattered by the
winds of heaven, the impartial voice of future
times will rejudge your verdict'*.

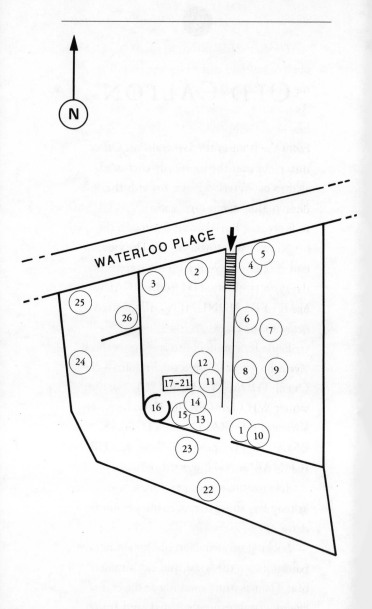

OLD CALTON CEMETERY

The foundation stone of the 90 feet obelisk was laid in 1844 as some 400 members of the Complete Suffrage Association, dressed from head to foot in black, walked past the High Court and covered the entire side of the Calton Hill, menacing in mourning. Robert Burns is said to have been so moved at the injustice done that he composed 'Scots Wha Hae' in honour of the Political Martyrs.

Now, as you climb the steep steps, you emerge from street-level into the light of day. Graves are shoulder-high to right and left of you. On the far right the grey stone drum of the David Hume monument strikes you immediately, framing the pensive bronze statue of President Abraham Lincoln (the first statue of him in Europe) which stands tall above a freed slave green with patina. Up on the far left huddles what remains of the hated Calton Jail— the turrets of the old governor's house.

Imagine for a moment a typical funeral at the time of Sir Walter Scott. He describes how 'the funeral pomp set forth —saulies [hired mourners] with their batons and gumphions [funeral banners] of tarnished white crêpe. Six starved horses, themselves the very emblems of mortality, well cloaked and plumed, lugging along the hearse with its dismal emblazonry, creep in slow pace towards the place of enterment, preceded by Jamie the idiot who, with weepers [strips of muslin stitched onto the edges of the sleeves of his black coat] and cravat made of white paper, attended every funeral and followed by six mourning coaches filled with the company'.

When you have reached the top of the first set of steps, turn back and look over the road to what is left of the rest of the burial ground after Waterloo Place was driven through the east end of Princes Street to Regent Road. Some gravestones are left beside what was once the main entrance to the burial ground.

Then climb the second set of steps onto the pink-chipped pathway, step to the right and walk back over the grass towards Waterloo Place. Near the retaining wall is a gravestone to a local Calton tradesman, one of many who used to fill the district with bustle and noise. The inscription reads: 'Here lyes the body of [2] **THOMAS MYLNE**, Smith in Calton, who died on the 12th June 1770 aged 31 years'. At the top of the stone you can see the crown of honour and the hammer of his trade [metalworker and tinsmith].

Turn left towards the far-off statue of the Duke of Wellington on his horse. The facing wall holds the imposing monument to [3] **JOHN MORTON**, (*d* 1739 aged 61), fashionable hatmaker in the burgh of

Calton. On top is the face of an angel
framed by its wings—this is the so-called
'winged soul', the soul departing the body
at the moment of death. On each side are
two plump women holding up a book—
symbolising the fruitfulness of the Word
of God (trade and piety went very much
hand in hand).

Now go back in the direction you came
and cross over the central path to the other
side, walking back towards the same wall
over Waterloo Place. Look at the pretty
headstone of [4] **ELIZABETH WILKIE**
(*d* 1747) and [5] **THOMAS GRAY** (*d*
1732), wright (carpenter) in a busy
Pleasance workshop. At the back of the
stone are the square and compass—the
symbols of Freemasonry. The stone was
erected by their son, Captain John Gray,
and shows a full-masted galleon (with
castles on its three masts) straining in the
wind, carving a foaming wake through the
heaving sea. Below are three-dimensional
thigh-bones, a skull, a monstrous bearded
man's head and that of a woman wearing a
wide lace collar—these are probably the
masonic emblems of the sun and moon.
Carved delicately into the stone is a small
anchor. You can almost smell the salt
spray.

Turn back up the grass slope toward
the Martyrs obelisk, passing to the left a

sunken crowned winged head softly mouth-
ing the message *'Memento Mori'* (*'Remember
you will die'*). Luxuriant laurel bushes and
ivy cover many of the walled graves behind.

Now we come to three theatricals—
perhaps you can smell the greasepaint or
hear the faint sound of applause? To the
right is the reverse side of the pink granite slabstone of {6} **JAMES LUMSDEN**
(1836-99), couthy singer of Scots songs,
whose annual Lumsden Burns Festivals
packed the Usher Hall year after year with
fans eager to enjoy a nostalgic whiff of the
Highlands. Next, behind you, listen to
the sonorous tones of the tragic actor {7}
WILLIAM WOODS (1749-1802) who
trod the creaking boards at the nearby
Theatre Royal in many a stirring leading
role, tugging at the heartstrings. Then
comes the grey granite obelisk to {8}
CHARLES MACKAY (1787-1857),
gritty star of the old Theatre Royal (on the
site of the present GPO). Mackay was a
character actor who caused a sensation in
1819 as Bailie Nicol Jarvie in Sir Walter
Scott's 'Rob Roy'. Even Scott was bowled
over by Mackay's performance: 'he seemed
to bring more out of it than I ever put in.
I was electrified by the truth, spirit and
humour which he threw into it'.

Just before you reach the Martyrs
Monument you pass on your left the

square, eight foot pillar commemorating members of the Williamson family. You will know you are there by the muffled Indian war-cry in the air, for beside the pillar lies the body of [9] **PETER WILLIAMSON** ('Indian Peter') (1730-99), stolen from the pier at Aberdeen when only eight and sold into slavery in Philadelphia. Scalped by Red Indians, he used his knowledge of survival in the wild to escape and enlist in the army fighting against the Indians.

When he retired to Edinburgh, (scalped head and all), he opened a popular tavern and coffeehouse beside St Giles. Then he moved into bookselling, printing and publishing. He even organised the first Penny Post and street directory in Edinburgh (1773). Indian Peter was one of the most famous, colourful, argumentative figures about town, always ready to tell a hair-raising tale or two of life on the run.

Can you smell a mysterious attractive scent where you are standing? To the left of the base of the Martyrs obelisk is the handsome Greek temple grave of the elegant perfumer [10] **WILLIAM RAE-BURN** (*d* 1812) who sent many a young Edinburgh belle to the city's dances on the sweetest of breezes.

Face to your right looking towards the statue of Abraham Lincoln. To the far left is a fine view of Edinburgh Castle; hard to your right, through a gap in the buildings, you can see out past Leith, over the Firth of Forth to the hills of Fife. Straight in front of you, over the top of the slabstone of {11} **THOMAS WHYTE** (a Calton baker), with its echo of warm loaves early in the morning, is a round white plaque with the profile of the historical painter {12} **DAVID ALLAN** (1744-96), winner in Rome of the St Luke gold medal for composition. Allan was director of the prestigious Edinburgh Trustees Academy (art school).

Beside him is the grave of a shoemaker (*d* 1762), identifiable by the symbols of a crown above a half-moon knife, recalling the smell of cut and polished leather and the crack of the hammer.

Walk back a little to enable you to step down onto the central path. Go forward towards the Martyrs obelisk. Just before you reach the obelisk, turn right up the four little steps to David Hume's monument, passing the walled grave of {13} **ALEXANDER REID** (*d* 1788). In front of you is the tablestone of {14} **ROBERT HOLMES,** a Belfast merchant who died on a visit to the city in 1808. Go left round the Hume monument to the wall and look over to the High Street. You are at the grave of {15} **WILLIAM**

GIBSON (*d* 1807), Assistant Superinten-
dent of Mail Coaches—'The bright
example of a generous mind'—whose
vehicles clattered in and out of the city in
all weathers, bringing packets, parcels,
love-letters and bills.

You are now beside the **[16] DAVID
HUME** (1711-76) monument. It is open
to the elements like a roofless Scottish
'broch', with a single fragile tree sprouting
leaves behind the iron spikes and bars of
the gate. It is designed as a monument to
a man who was warm-hearted, sympath-
etic and kind, but one who could not
believe either in God or in an afterlife. He
was punished for his atheism by the Church
authorities of his day who blocked his
appointment to University teaching posts.

Groundless rumours that Hume had
made a pact with the Devil were taken so
seriously by his many friends that after his
funeral they kept a constant watch over
his grave, eight of them guarding the
tomb every evening, firing pistols and
lighting candles in lanterns placed on the
grave. They kept this up for eight nights
after his funeral.

Standing 15 feet from the ground is
the commanding life-size figure of the
American President Abraham Lincoln,
freeing the slave who sits below among the
flags of battle, lifting his hand in gratitude.

Here also are the graves of five Scotsmen who died in the American Civil War (1861-65)—[17] Sergeant Major **JOHN McEWAN** of the 65th Illinois Volunteer Rifles; [18] Lieutenant Colonel **WILLIAM DUFF** of the 2nd Illinois Artillery; [19] **ROBERT STEEDMAN** of the 5th Maine Infantry Volunteers; [20] **JAMES WILKIE** of the 1st Michigan Cavalry and [21] **ROBERT FERGUSON** of the 57th New York Infantry Volunteers.

Return to the central path and go beyond the base of the Political Martyrs Monument towards the High Street. Facing you is the iron-studded door of [22] **DANIEL STEWART**'s tomb, the founder of Daniel Stewart's Hospital. Stewart (1741-1814) worked at the Scottish Exchequer in Parliament Square for 43 years and died unmarried. He never forgot those less well-off than himself (he was born into poverty in Perthshire). With the money that he left, Daniel Stewart's Hospital (now College), designed by David Rhind, was built in Queensferry Road.

Turn right down the granite-chipped path. Beside you on the right is the flat stone which marks the final resting-place of [23] **JULIUS VON YELLIN**, an unfortunate member of the Royal Academy of Munich who was 'seized with illness'

while addressing the Royal Society of
Edinburgh in 1826. He went to bed in
the Royal Hotel and never got up again.

Walk on down and follow the path as
it bears right below the back of the Hume
monument. As you go down onto the grass
you will see in front of you to the left the
unmarked walled grave of the sculptor,
[24] Sir **JOHN STEELL** (1804-91), its
black iron mortsafe bursting with spotted
yellow laurel bushes, an ancient and empty
gas light-fitting jutting above your head.
Steel was responsible for most of the finest
statues in Edinburgh—for example, the
seated figure of Queen Victoria on the
Royal Scottish Academy (1844); Sir
Walter Scott under the Scott Monument
(1840-46); the Duke of Wellington on
horse-back (1852); Allan Ramsay above
the Floral Clock (1865); and Prince Albert
in Charlotte Square (1876) among others.
Queen Victoria was so pleased with her
husband's statue that she knighted Steell
at Holyrood.

Ironically, every trace of John Steell has
been erased from his grave—the once-
locked gate swings open, the wall where a
plaque should be is scarred and pitted by
the elements. The man who spent most of
his working life making monuments to
others has no memorial to himself. His is
a grave with no name.

Facing you further on in a quiet leafy corner is the elaborate grave of the publisher, [25] **WILLIAM BLACKWOOD** (1776-1834), town councillor, founder of the Tory *Blackwood's Magazine,* which only ceased publication in 1976. From his august premises at 25 George Street, he published many of the finest writers in his '*Maga*', as well as other works including the *New Statistical Account* (1840). On each side of the ornamental gate, torches flame upside down in mourning.

Turn to your right and you see on the far wall the bronze profile of another great Edinburgh publisher, [26] **ARCHIBALD CONSTABLE** (1774-1827), tall, bluff and hearty, the genial open-handed bookseller who published the *Scots Magazine* from 1801, bought up the *Encyclopaedia Britannica* and published the works of Sir Walter Scott. After moving into a new shop at 10 Princes Street, Constable planned to serialise Scott's 'Waverley Novels', but in 1826 his London agents went bankrupt dragging Constable with them, in turn ruining Walter Scott. Sadly Constable ended his life in ill-health and bitter disappointment.

7

NEW CALTON

Walk on down towards the Burns Monument which commands a view of the Firth of Forth. Beyond the monument turn right, down into the New Calton Burial Ground.

If Old Calton lies high above the heads of the passers-by then New Calton does the reverse—it falls away from you as you enter, a long sloping field. As you go in you see on your right the watchtower (boarded up). From the gate there is a good view of Holyrood Palace with its roofless Abbey and gold-tipped turrets.

Turn right towards the watchtower. When you get there, turn to face the Firth of Forth where it opens into the North Sea. Walk forward ten paces down the right side of a low wall. Perhaps you can hear a distant bosun's whistle, canvas flapping in the wind or the groaning of ship's timbers? New Calton was once known as 'the cemetery of the admirals'—at least five are buried here: for example, Rear Admiral Andrew Smith (*d* 1831). Go ahead and turn left down the steps. Follow the line of graves to your left—the second grave is that of {1} Vice Admiral **ALEXANDER**

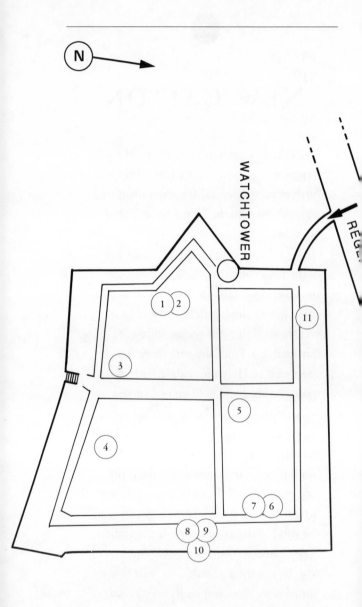

NEW CALTON CEMETERY

FRASER (*d* 1829) and [2] Vice Admiral
THOMAS FRASER (*d* 1870).

Walk on over the grass to reach the
path. Turn right and walk down it. At the
end of the wall to your right is the red
granite stone of gruff [3] **DAVID BRYCE**
(1803-76), architect of the Royal Infirmary,
Fettes College and the Bank of Scotland
headquarters. Bryce worked right up to
his death from bronchitis.

Walk on down the path again towards
the Canongate, down to the bottom of the
steps and turn left. Just before reaching the
large tree, turn back left again up the slope.

On your right is the broken white
pillar marking the honoured grave of [4]
ANDREAS GREGOROWICZ, Polish
lawyer, surgeon, soldier and freedom-
fighter who died in 1838 aged 31. Having
fought as a student against the Russians
he escaped to Edinburgh where he began
training as a surgeon. Within a year he
was dead from an attack of plague contracted while attending the poor of the city.

Continue back up the slope. When you
reach the path, again turn left and then
first right at the next intersection. Walk
up the slope for ten paces—on your right
is the red granite headstone of the farrier
[5] **WILLIAM DICK** (1793-1866) born
in White Horse Close beside the coaching-
stables. Dick developed veterinary science

in Edinburgh and in 1823 founded the Dick College, becoming a Professor of Edinburgh University in 1844.

Walk on to the end of the path and at the T-junction turn right. Walk down to where the path turns right under a large tree at the far end of the burial ground and follow it. Immediately on your right is the fine red granite stone of {6} **WILLIAM MacGILLIVRAY** (1796-1852), Professor of Natural History in Aberdeen, author of *A History of British Birds*. At the foot of the stone is a bronze plaque of the King of Birds—an eagle waiting for its prey, full of power and noble aggression.

Beside it, by contrast, is the grave of poor {7} **ROBERT MACKERTER** who spent 50 years in the service of the Earls of Haddington and died in 1841 aged 78 ('*Zeal, Fidelity and Attachment*'), self-effacing by trade.

The fifth walled grave to your left is full of the smell of the sea. Here lie {8} **ROBERT STEVENSON** (1772-1850) and his sons {9} **THOMAS** (1818-87) and {10} **ALAN** (1807-65). Robert Stevenson, grandfather of Robert Louis Stevenson, studied engineering and worked for the Northern Lighthouse Board, overseeing the construction of twenty lighthouses, shining over the sea, through fog and storm. He invented intermittent and flashing lights, so much a feature of the lighthouse as we know it. His greatest achievement was the Bell Rock Lighthouse, built on a dangerous reef in the North Sea. Stevenson also had great influence on the shape of Edinburgh as we know it—he engineered Waterloo Place, supervised the construction of London Road, designed the Calton Jail, drained the Nor' Loch to make Princes St Gardens and planned Granton Harbour.

His son Alan built 10 lighthouses including the Skerryvore 14 miles into the Atlantic. Thomas Stevenson, father of Robert Louis, was a specialist in light-house illumination.

The visit to New Calton cemetery now over, turn back uphill towards the gate. Just before you reach the gates spare a glance to the right at the square pillar with its crudely-carved skull and cross-bones, the grave of one [11] **JAMES STRACHAN,** humble tanner in his reeking dye-baths at Canonmills.

And as you exit by the gates, pause at the elaborately-decorated shoemaker's grave with winged soul in free flight, winking skulls, scrolls and that familiar sly whispered message—'*Memento Mori*'.

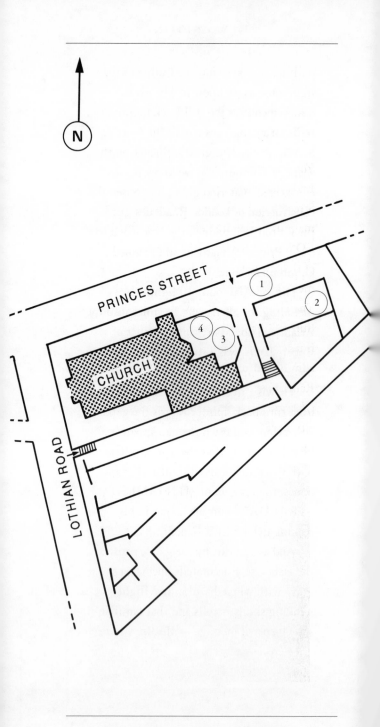

ST JOHN'S CHURCHYARD

8

ST JOHN'S

You enter the church of St John's (West
End) at the gate opposite South Charlotte
Street. There you pass on your left the
magnificent white Celtic cross to {1} Dean
EDWARD RAMSAY (1793-1872), one
of the few people in Edinburgh to have a
memorial erected by public subscription.
The Dean was a well-loved figure, a fine
flute-player, a bell-ringing expert, a
financial wizard, who presided over the
administration of St John's for 44 years.
Ramsay's *Reminiscences of Scottish Life and
Character* preserved a fund of anecdotes of
city life and valuable examples of the Scots
tongue for posterity.

DEAN RAMSAY

Walk down the slope for a few feet and then bear sharp left into a burial enclosure. On the far right, set into a low wall almost hidden from view is the red granite stone of [2] **JAMES SYME** (1799-1870), known as the 'Napoleon of Surgery', the greatest surgeon of his day, who trained and practised in Edinburgh. One of his house-surgeons described vividly the working life of Syme, the Professor of Clinical Surgery: 'Two lectures a week, operations two days more, a ward visit when he wished to see any special cases. He spent generally about two hours in the hospital … '

He was also a popular lecturer, with 'students racing to get to the nearest seats in the large operating theatre … '

Go back the way you came. Walk up the slope and turn left up to the 'Dorm-itory' garden attached to the back of the church. Facing you is the small white stone to [3] **ANNE RUTHERFORD** (1732-1819)—Sir Walter Scott's mother.

Now walk to your right. In the middle of the wall, smothered in white and yellow roses, is the grave of artist [4] Sir **HENRY RAEBURN** (1756-1823), son of a yarn-boiler. His father died when Raeburn was only six and he was sent to Heriot's Hospital. After his schooldays he was apprenticed to a goldsmith and jeweller in Parliament Square.

One day the seal engraver David Deuchar came to the shop and noticed the young apprentice quickly hiding something he was working on—a copy of a miniature painting which had been sent in for repair. The copy was excellent and Deuchar engaged him to make more. He then introduced Raeburn to the painter David Martin who helped him in his study of art—Raeburn's only training.

Raeburn's elder brother had taken over his father's business in Stockbridge and there Raeburn met the Countess of Leslie, Ann Edgar, whose husband had recently died. He painted her portrait and fell in love with her. They married and he settled into a comfortable life as a man of means at the house of Deanhaugh.

Although bankrupted in 1807 by the failure of a family business, Raeburn owned a considerable amount of land in the Stockbridge area of the city and built Raeburn Place, Ann Street and Leslie Place.

Knighted by George IV at Hopetoun House in 1822, Henry Raeburn died the following year after catching a chill on an archaeological visit to Fife.

Raeburn's great gift was his ability to 'plunge at once through all the constraint and embarrassment of the sitter and present the face, clear, open, and intelligent as at the most disengaged moments'.

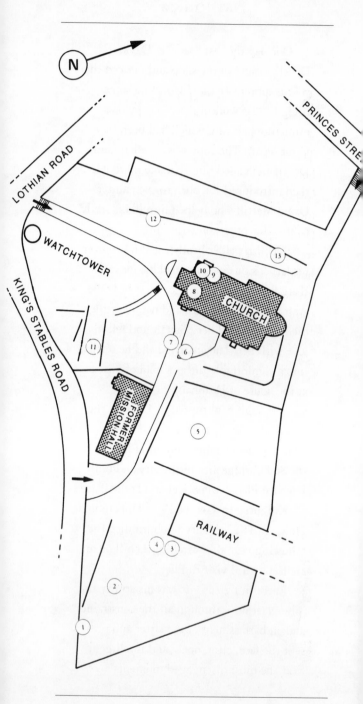

ST CUTHBERT'S CHURCHYARD

9

ST CUTHBERT'S

The site of St Cuthbert's Church has been holy ground since the Dark Ages. Cuthbert (AD 635-87), born in East Lothian, was a monk at Melrose and later Bishop of Lindisfarne. Tradition has it that he came up from Melrose and pitched his tent in the hollow ground below the Castle, so giving his name to the first church built outside the walls of the fortress.

ST CUTHBERT'S CHURCH

In the churchyard there are no pre-Reformation monuments—first mention of a graveyard came in 1595 when the small hill to the south-west of the church ('the Knowe'), which previously had been used to graze sheep, horses and cattle, was enclosed by a stone wall.

Being so far from the safety of the Old Town, St Cuthbert's was an easy target for the Resurrectionists, the corpse-stealers. In 1738 the problem became so serious that the walls of the churchyard were raised to eight feet. Two years later the Kirk Session appointed an officer to keep records of the dead and a lodge on the site of the present watchtower was used as an office for the 'recorder'.

But grave-diggers were still being bribed to leave the gates of the church-yard unlocked and the graves prised open with specially-designed crowbars.

Enter the cemetery by the gate from King's Stables Road, turn half right and go diagonally to the end of the wall near-est you, which runs from the small lodge to your right, parallel to the boundary wall. Walk past the last grave on the wall-end (James Millar), and turn right along it. Follow the wall from the grave of John Forres to the 24th monument: there, under a tall street-lamp, lies [1] Mrs **ANNE GRANT** of Laggan (1755-1838).

Anne Grant lived at the end of Loch Ness, inside the high bastion walls of Fort Augustus where her father was barrack-master. In 1779 she married the minister of Laggan who was also chaplain to the Fort. After 20 years of marriage her husband died, leaving her with eight children.

Her time in Laggan, deep in the central Highlands near the River Spey, was well spent. She learned Gaelic and studied the language and customs of the Highlands. The romantic Scottish scenery is lovingly described in her *Letters from the Mountains,* written during her 30 years there.

In 1810 Mrs Grant moved to Edinburgh where she stayed until her death.

Now trace your steps back again. At the eleventh grave on your right is the large Celtic cross dedicated to the artist [2] **ALEXANDER NASMYTH** (1758-1840) who was born in the Grassmarket in the shadow of the Castle.

As a boy he loved clambering up the steep south side of the Castle Rock. His early years were spent at the High School after which he was apprenticed to a coach-builder. But he soon showed his artistic talent, painting the side-panels of the finest carriages, and he took further art training at the Trustees Academy. Then Nasmyth was hired by Allan Ramsay, the portrait painter, to work in London colouring in the backgrounds and clothes in Ramsay's portraits.

He returned to Edinburgh in 1778 and constructed his own house and studio at 47 York Place.

Nasmyth helped design Telford's Dean Bridge and also drew up plans for the dazzling Temple of Hygeia over St Bernard's Well close to the Water of Leith. He was best known for his 'bow and string' bridge which was used all over Britain.

Nasmyth's elder son Patrick was the painter known as 'the father of Scottish landscape'; his youngest son James was the inventor of the steam-hammer.

Now turn towards the railway cutting in front of you on the right. Under the trees you see the tall monument to the lawyer [3] **ROBERT JAMESON** (1784-1834), a sculptured memorial by Sir John Steell in the Greek style, showing a young man protecting a child from a mysterious threatening figure behind.

Jameson's skill as a lawyer and his honesty had made him one of the leading figures of his day in the Scottish courts. But early death meant that his promise remained unfulfilled. The Faculty of Advocates paid for the handsome monument as a mark of their respect.

On the other side of the monument is the grave of Robert's father (although

with a different spelling of the surname)
[4] Revd **JOHN JAMIESON** (1759-1838)
who holds a special place in Scottish
history for having preserved much of our
traditions and language in his *Etymological
Dictionary of the Scottish Language* (1808-9).

Now go towards the black street-lamp
at the back of the former Mission Hall,
beside the gate you came in by. Just before
you get there, turn half right into the
large grassy enclosure. Walk 32 paces into
the centre of the grass. Here is the monument to [5] **GEORGE MEIKLE KEMP**
(1795-1844), the shy, brilliant designer of
the Scott Monument, whose own coffin
was accompanied by over 1000 people.

Kemp's death was a tragedy
out of the blue. He had gone to
visit the contractor at his office
beside the Union Canal Basin
to check on the supply of stone
on the evening of 6th March
1844. The night was very
foggy and dark. Kemp left
the contractor and set off
down the towpath along
the Canal—a favourite
walk of his.

He lost his bearing in
the dark, became confused, took the
wrong path and fell off the pier near the
Lochrin Distillery into the icy waters of

The
SCOTT
MONUMENT

the canal. Although an expert swimmer, he seemed to have been sucked down into the mud at the bottom.

It was not till a week later that his body was found. A thorn walking-stick was the first clue to appear. Then his hat floated to the surface—he always wore it securely attached by a cord to his coat—and so the body was discovered.

Rumours began to spread that he had been drunk, or had committed suicide through depression, or some jealous rival in the Scott Monument competition had attacked him. There was no evidence at all for any of this.

It was expected that Kemp would be buried under the Scott Monument. However this proved to be impossible. Today he lies with a glimpse of his masterpiece through the trees across Princes Street Gardens.

Walk towards the bright red door of the church now, out past the wall which surrounds the central enclosure you have been in. As you emerge you see on your right a triangular plot of ground shaded by a large weeping tree. Facing you is a sandstone obelisk. Listen for the music of the organ, for this is the grave of [6] the Revd **ROBERT SMITH** (1780-1829), composer of the hymn 'How beautiful upon the mountains', former choirmaster of Paisley Abbey and musical director of St George's Parish Church.

Can you hear the soft sighing of a distant violin? Perhaps it is because you are close to the memorial stone of {7} **GIROLAMO STABILINI** (1761-1815), violinist and teacher. His grave is at the level of the path, set into the retaining wall to your left.

Born in the hot backstreets of Rome, Stabilini came to Edinburgh in 1783, a talented young man invited by the directors of the Musical Society of Edinburgh who were anxious to find a new leader for their orchestra. Stabilini soon became undisputed king of the Edinburgh concerts.

He joined Lodge Canongate Kilwinning No 2. Robert Burns, a fellow mason, attended a number of Stabilini's concerts and evidently enjoyed them. Stabilini also joined the Royal Edinburgh Volunteers and liked to go to Leith Races, on one occasion injuring his precious 'bowing-arm' there. He was open, friendly, happy go lucky, with a fatal taste for good wine.

For Stabilini's career was being slowly affected by his enjoyment of the good things in life. He died of dropsy and his body had to be carried on a door by his friends, feet first out of his Rose Street lodgings.

Go to the main door of the church. On

the back wall to your right is the magnificently-carved monument to [8] **JOHN NAPIER** (1550-1617). Napier was born at Merchiston Castle (now incorporated into Napier Polytechnic at Colinton Road). His father was Master of the Scottish Mint. Napier studied at St Andrews and travelled widely on the Continent.

He was fascinated by astronomy, mathematics, alchemy and astrology and had a reputation for wizardry because of his uncanny powers over the natural world. He was a loner and was often seen walking in the evenings, dressed in a long cloak, accompanied by his large black dog.

Napier was a staunch supporter of the Reformed Church, throwing himself with tremendous energy and imagination into theology and science. In 1588 he was a Commissioner for the Presbytery of Edinburgh at the General Assembly. In 1593 he published *A Plaine Discovery of the Whole Revelation of St John,* strongly critical of the Roman Church.

Napier is better known, however, for a series of practical military, industrial and agricultural inventions—for example, a tank; a powerful land mirror for setting fire to ships at sea; artillery capable of firing in every direction; a hydraulic screw for clearing flooded mine-workings and a variety of new methods of farming.

But it was his invention of Logarithms in 1617 (a technique of calculation using rods or bones carved with numbers) which made him an outstanding figure in the history of mathematics, an early pioneer in the development of the computer and helped to lay the mathematical foundations which made the Industrial Revolution of 1750 possible.

Standing in the church you may catch a whiff of scent on the air, hear the rustle of silk and a woman's musical laugh. Near you, close beneath the memorial plaque to [9] Sir **JAMES ROCHEAD** (1666-1737), beside the far staircase in the church, is the burial-place of [10] Mrs **JANET ROCHEAD** (1725-90), one of Edinburgh's most elegant women.

Janet Watson of Muirhouse married Alexander Rochead in 1750 and went to live in the family home of Inverleith House (the present Royal Botanic Garden), with its avenue of trees and shaded glades. Her husband died five years later.

She is remembered with amazement by Lord Henry Cockburn—'she would sail like a ship from Tarshish, gorgeous in velvet or rustling in silk, done up in all the accompaniments of fan, ear-rings, finger-rings, falling sleeves, scent bottle, embroidered bag, hoop and train—all superb, yet all in purest taste …'

Leave the church and rejoin the retaining wall around the Knowe (higher ground). Walk along the wall beyond the church tower. When you reach the steps on your left go up them, following the path as it curves towards the right. To the left are walled tombs, devastated and crumbling, the roofs open to the sky.

Now on your right *'Memento Mori'* catches your eye under a 'winged soul' with a broken nose. Continue along the path. Knee-high, two hollow-eyed skulls sit at either end of a long leg-bone. Pass carefully round the end of the tombs and up the small incline behind.

Go to the eighth grave against the wall. The headstone has a semi-circular top and tells you that here lies the brilliant English author {11} **THOMAS De QUINCEY** (1785-1859), the mysterious 'Opium-Eater'.

THOMAS
DE QUINCEY

Through the ragged stones and peaty earth of the walled grave to the left are the twisted roots of ancient trees locked into a pointed obelisk and surmounted by the rusted standard of a long-dead gas-lamp. Above it, all you see is the steeple of St Cuthbert's and its clock with the golden hands.

De Quincey was a Manchester boy

educated in Bath where he became fluent in both Latin and Greek by the age of 15. He was sent to Manchester Grammar School but ran away to Wales and began a life of wandering the hills, living off his charm and writing business and love-letters for his hosts. Then he went to London, falling foul of money-lenders, and took to wandering the streets, lonely and penniless. But with his family's help De Quincey was sent to Oxford. It was in Oxford that he first took opium for tooth-ache. He was to leave Oxford without a degree.

De Quincey admired the poems of Wordsworth and Coleridge and set out to the Lake District to meet them. In the Lakes he met up with the muscular literary rogue, John Wilson, the author—alias 'Christopher North'—editor of *Blackwood's Magazine*.

De Quincey made two visits to Edinburgh with Wilson, the first in 1813. He found refuge in the Debtors' Sanctuary at Holyrood, from which he emerged in the evenings to fascinate the literary men of the city with his racy conversation which sparkled brightest after midnight when his imagination was afire.

Back in his Lake District cottage De Quincey continued to take opium, taking as much as 320 grains a day in 1813.

However, he managed to cut down, felt much better and married the 18 year old daughter of a local farmer.

Twelve months later he was deep into drugs again. This is the period of his life he describes in his *Confessions of an Opium Eater* (1822).

Looking for work and a place of refuge he settled in Edinburgh in 1828 and stayed there until his death.

Now go back the way you came. Go down the steps towards the church and then make straight for the long wall of graves facing you. Go to the fourth grave from the far left of the wall to the resting-place of [12] **ADAM ROLLAND** (1734-1819) of Gask, Principal Clerk of Session, just touched by the branches of a giant tree.

People used to stop and stare at the advocate Adam Rolland. He cut an odd figure. Lord Cockburn described him thus: 'his dresses, which were changed at least twice every day, were always of the same old beau cut. The vicissitudes of fashion being contemptible in the sight of a person who had made up his own mind as to the perfection of a gentleman's outward covering. The favourite hues were black and mulberry; the stuffs—velvet, fine kerseymere and satin. When all got up no artificial rose could be brighter or stiffer. He was like one of the creatures come to life again in a collection of dried butterflies'.

Walk on to the twenty-fourth grave on the wall at your right. It has five knobbly Gothic pinnacles against the sky. Did you perhaps glimpse a dark, tall, striking young woman walking past you? It may have been the novelist [13] **SUSAN FERRIER** (1782-1854), a very attractive personality whose conversation sparkled with humour and intelligence.

Now you may leave the churchyard by the steps up onto Lothian Road—to your left—past the newly-restored watchtower gleaming in the sun.

The OLD CHURCH of ST CUTHBERT'S
and the NOR' LOCH

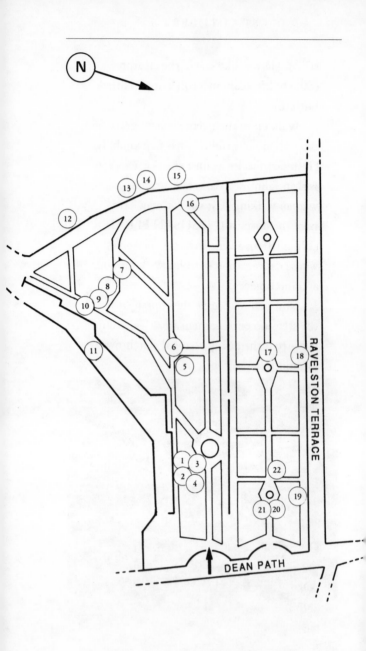

DEAN CEMETERY

10

DEAN

The gnarled stone pillars of the main gate, pyramids balanced on top, the glimpse of trimmed green-and-gold holly bushes mixed with ancient yews reveal that you are in the most elegant of all Edinburgh cemeteries.

As you pass through the heavy black gates turn first left and then first right. Walk past nine Celtic crosses (white, pink and grey granite). On your left is a glorious wilderness—birds sing in the treetops and below is the valley of the secret river Dean with the spires of city churches pointing to the sky.

Continue along the path until you see a large pink granite obelisk on your right with a green bronze classical head on top, its eyes stained black, its beard flowing. This is the grave of two fine artists—[1] **DAVID OCTAVIUS HILL** (1802-70) the photographic pioneer, and his wife [2] **AMELIA R PATON** (1820-1904), the sculptor who made the bronze head of her husband.

Imagine the soft click of the shutter on Hill's camera or the agony of his sitters, posing rock-still for minutes on end, their heads and arms locked by invisible metal cramps. Imagine the sun dazzling his eyes as he squints through the old-fashioned lens?

Hill (originally a painter) worked with his associate Robert Adamson on the flat roof of his home in Rock House at the Calton Hill taking 'sun-pictures' (*calotypes*), and in the fishing villages by the Forth, making atmospheric portraits with the new chemical mysteries of photography. His own masterpiece captured 'The Free Church of Scotland' (1843-66), studies for which he made with portrait photographs.

Now walk to your right over the grass to the tall Celtic cross, fantastic animals woven together in perfect symmetry. Designed by his brother William it commemorates the painter [3] **DAVID SCOTT** (1807-49), trained in Italy. His green bronze head above the cross weeps a long black tear. Scott, a brilliant but unfashionable painter, lived a lonely and embittered life in the family home of Hermits and Termits at St Leonards.

Close by is the grave of [4] **ROBERT ANSTRUTHER** (1823-95) doctor, Arctic explorer and traveller who sailed in 1849 to look for the ill-fated Franklin Expedition. Again, the following year, he took part in the continued search organised by Lady Franklin. Can you hear the howl of the

Arctic wind and the creaking of the ice?
Can you feel the frost-bite at your fingers?

Escape to the path and walk quickly
on. Trimmed into enormous dark living
monuments, yew and holly trees tower
ominously above you. Peep over the parapet
wall to your left. There is the Water of
Leith slipping between knotted and
twisted trunks. Make towards the black
obelisk straight ahead. As you approach it,
just before the second path leading to the
right you can catch your breath in front of
the stylish headstone to the bearded and
bohemian artist [5] **SAM BOUGH** (1822-
78). Below is a bronze palette, brushes and
oil-paints.

Now walk to the foot of the enormous
obelisk dedicated to the six officers and
369 NCOs and men of the [6] **79th
HIGHLANDERS** who died in Bulgaria
and in the Crimean War (1854-55) at the
battles of Alma and Sevastopol. Also
commemorated are the five officers and
343 NCOs who died in India (1857-71).

Continue past the obelisk and take the
first turning on the left. Walk forward
until you reach another large blunt obelisk
on your left to [7] **JOHN WILSON** (1800-
49), the famous Scottish tenor. Turn left
round the obelisk and go along the path
which takes a slow curve towards the right.
When you reach the T-junction look right.

A weird grey pagan carving looms at you like a bad dream—three winged lions under three rams heads, and a column above surrounded by three pelicans, ending in a flat dish high above—this is the unsettling gravestone of {8} **JOHN LEISHMAN**, WS (1801-61), and {9} Brigadier-General **OFFLEY SHORE** (1866-1922).

Then on your left across the path is the modest headstone of {10} **HENRY D LITTLEJOHN** (1826-1914), the city's first Medical Officer of Health (1862), who dramatically reduced the cases of typhus and smallpox in the city. Dr Littlejohn was the man responsible for the *Report on the City Cemeteries* (1883).

Continue up the path past a quietly weeping woman, take the first hidden path to your left and walk down between holly and rhododendron for 100 paces. At the second angle of the wall on your left is a magnificent Celtic cross, the last resting-place of the painter of fairies and medieval fantasy, {11} Sir **JOHN NOEL PATON** (1821-1901).

Turn back and retrace your steps. As you reach the top of the path, again walk straight forward towards the large pink granite pyramid in the distance.

Eight plots on is the white marble monument to {12} **ALEXANDER MONRO** *Tertius* (1773-1859), the last in the dynasty of grandfather, father and son who collectively held the Chair of Surgery in Edinburgh for 125 years. Monro *Tertius* was not, however, a particularly exciting teacher—he used to read from his grandfather's lecture notes word for word!

Nineteen plots further on is the grave of the lawyer {13} **HENRY COCKBURN** (1779-1854) with its Gothic stonework and bronze profile. Cockburn defended Thomas Burke's wife in the Burke and Hare Resurrectionist trial of 1828, helped to draft the first Scottish Electoral Reform Bill, founded the Edinburgh Academy and the Commercial Bank, and was Solicitor General for Scotland. He loved nature and the environment and is best summed up by *The Edinburgh Review* (to which he often contributed), as 'rather below the middle height, firm, wiry and muscular, inured to active exercise of all kinds, a good swimmer, and accomplished skater and an intense lover of the breezes of heaven. He was the model of a high-bred Scotch gentleman …'

Next to it is the plain white altar to the architect {14} **WILLIAM PLAYFAIR** (1789-1857) who designed many of the city's best-known buildings—the National Gallery and the Royal Scottish Academy at the Mound, the National Monument on Calton Hill, and Surgeons' Hall.

Beyond is the raised table-altar to [15]
FRANCIS JEFFREY (1773-1850), Lord
Advocate and founder of the influential
Edinburgh Review (1802) at his Buccleuch
Place flat.

Walk forward till you meet a dark
green Celtic cross which tells the moving
story of [16] Lt **JOHN IRVING** RN
(1815-1848/49) who left England under
Sir John Franklin in May 1845 on the
HMS 'Terror', on an expedition to find the
North West Passage to the Pacific. They
wintered at Beechey Island and then sailed
south down Franklin's Strait, entering the
North West Passage. For two years they
were locked in the ice. Sir John Franklin,
some officers and 15 seamen died. The
105 survivors (Irving among them), landed on King William's Land and tried to
march into Canada, but every one of them
died from cold and want of food. They
were so starved that they had begun to eat
their dead companions.

Thirty-three years later Lieutenant
Schwatka of the American Searching
Expedition discovered Irving's grave. His
remains were then returned to Britain.

Continue to the end of the path where
it meets the far wall. Turn right and walk
along to the opening in the wall to your
left. Go through the wall, turn left and
then first right. Walk towards the gigan-

tic pink obelisk to [17] **ALEXANDER RUSSEL** (1814-76), editor of *The Scotsman.* Go round the obelisk on the right and continue straight towards the boundary wall. As you reach the T-junction at the wall, look slightly left to the white marble cross facing you. This is the grave of [18] Dr **JOSEPH BELL** (1837-1911), the inspiration for Conan Doyle's world-famous detective, Sherlock Holmes.

As a young medical student at Edinburgh Conan Doyle was astonished by the deductive powers of his lecturer, Dr Bell. The author wrote in 1892 to his former teacher: 'It is most certainly to you that I owe Sherlock Holmes, although in the stories I have the advantage of being able to place him in all sorts of dramatic situations'.

Bell, however, was not so pleased with the comparison. In 1901 he wrote: 'Why bother … about the cataract of drivel for which Conan Doyle is responsible? I am sure he never imagined that such a heap of rubbish would fall on my devoted head in consequence of his stories!'

The *Strand Magazine* (in which the Holmes stories first appeared) quoted Conan Doyle as saying about Dr Bell, 'His intuitive powers were simply marvellous …'

Appointed early in life as Surgeon to the Royal Infirmary, Dr Bell retired and

was then made the first Surgeon to the
Sick Children's Hospital (then in Morningside Drive).

Now turn right down the path along
the side of the wall. Not long before the
end of the path there is a large dark green
obelisk on your right with a green bronze
bust of [19] Major General Sir **HECTOR
MACDONALD** (1853-1903), a figure of
mystery, a soldier so brilliant that he was
even rumoured to have risen from the dead!

'Fighting Mac' was born in Easter Ross,
son of a crofter. Enlisting as a private in
the 2nd Battalion of the Gordon Highlanders, he rose rapidly through the ranks
to become a colour sergeant.

During the Afghan campaigns he
performed spectacular acts of bravery and
leadership and he was offered the choice
between a Victoria Cross or a commission.
Despite the financial hardship, given the
expense of life in an officer's mess, Macdonald chose the commission and began
an equally meteoric rise as an officer of
outstanding ability. He joined the British-
controlled Egyptian army. He married at
Edinburgh Castle and subsequently was
transferred to South Africa where he dis-
tinguished himself against the Boers and
virtually saved the whole British army at
the Battle of Omdurman.

It was this last achievement which, it

is alleged, antagonised the future General
Kitchener and ended Sir Hector's career.
In dubious circumstances, he was accused
of homosexuality while in service in
Ceylon. On his way to London to answer
the charges, he booked into a Paris hotel
and was found soon afterwards in his room
shot through the head—apparently suicide.

In great secrecy, his coffin was taken to
the Dean cemetery—even the horses' hooves
were muffled—and buried at night.

Meanwhile rumours began to circulate
that the suicide found in Paris was not the
Major General and that his coffin had
been weighted with stones. For, by a
curious coincidence, his cousin Colonel
von Mackensen of the Prussian army had
passed away on the very same day in a
Berlin military hospital.

Months afterwards it was announced
that a terrible mistake had been made—
Colonel von Mackensen (the German form
of 'Mackenzie') was not dead after all: he
had only been seriously ill and had lost his
memory. He was now only able to speak
German with great difficulty.

Was Mackensen really Sir Hector Macdonald? Popular gossip thought so. For
from this time on von Mackensen seemed
to develop rather extraordinary military
skills and by the end of the Great War had
risen to the rank of Field Marshall and

then Commander-in-Chief of all German and Austrian armies at the Eastern Front.

Many years later, during the 1936 Berlin Olympics, von Mackensen was spotted sitting next to Hitler. And so the mystery of 'Fighting Mac' remains a tantalising possibility.

Continue down the path, following it as it turns right. As you reach the locked gates on your left, turn right up the broad path towards the tall Celtic cross. This is the monument to the Nasmyth family, a steam-hammer on one side and on the other the sword and broken hammers of the family crest. [20] **PATRICK NASMYTH** (1787-1831) and [21] **JAMES NASMYTH** (1808-90) and their wives are buried here. Both were sons of the famous painter Alexander Nasmyth (who is buried in St Cuthbert's).

Patrick Nasmyth followed his father's trade and became a landscape painter of note, fathering six daughters, all of whom were artists. James Nasmyth, 'engineer, astronomer and artist' as the monument says, helped to finance his studies at Edinburgh University by selling model steam-engines which he made in a small brass foundry in his bedroom. At 19 he designed and built a steam-car which ran up and down the Queensferry Road carrying eight passengers. He also invented a

steam-blast and a dinner oven and earned
himself a fairly comfortable existence.

In 1834 James Nasmyth established his
Bridgewater Factory at Manchester and six
years later designed his famous steam-
hammer which played such a key role in
the Industrial Revolution. After his retire-
ment in 1856 he turned to astronomy,
making telescopes.

Walk forwards towards the Russel
obelisk again. The ninth grave on your
right is the oceanographer [22] Sir **JOHN
MURRAY** (1841-1914). Born in Canada
of Scottish parents, he went to Edinburgh
University, first as a medical student, but
then taking a wide variety of subjects—
chemistry, law, natural history and
literature. At 27 he spent six months as a
surgeon on a whaler and worked on Jan
Mayen Island in the Greenland Sea. Later
he joined the Challenger Expedition to
the Antarctic and edited the results of the
Expedition, becoming director of the
Challenger office in 1876 (now Challenger
Lodge, a hospice for the terminally ill).

Murray was not only a marine zoologist
but a pioneer of modern oceanography,
surveying the Scottish freshwater lochs.
He also helped to found the Millport
biological laboratory and the Ben Nevis
Observatory.

WHO'S WHO
IN SELECTED
EDINBURGH GRAVEYARDS

BUCCLEUCH

Walking along Potterrow from the Old
Town you come to Chapel Street. To your
right is Buccleuch Parish Church (bound-
ed to the north by Windmill Lane), now
the property of Edinburgh University and
used as a store. Visitors to the cemetery
are free to enter during office hours.

In this cemetery you can find the
family grave of Dr **ANDREW DUNCAN**
(1744-1828), President of the Royal
College of Physicians and Professor of the
Theory of Medicine at Edinburgh. Duncan
was born in St Andrews, studied medicine
at Edinburgh and then worked as a ship's
surgeon for the East India Company. He
returned to Edinburgh and set up practice.
In his lifetime he founded many charitable
and useful organisations such as the Royal
Public Dispensary, the Caledonian Horti-
cultural Society and the Edinburgh
Lunatic Asylum (inspired apparently by
the unhappy death of young poet Robert
Fergusson who committed suicide in the
Edinburgh Bedlam). Dr Duncan himself is
commemorated in the Andrew Duncan
Clinic at Morningside.

Kind-hearted Duncan allowed one of his students to be buried here as well—**CHARLES DARWIN** (1758-78)—one of the celebrated scientific Darwins and a relative of the author of *Origin of the Species*.

Look out also for Mrs **ALISON RUTHERFORD** (or Cockburn) (1713-94) to whom a plaque on the other side of the wall in Chapel Street is dedicated.

She was a Border lass born near the River Tweed in Selkirkshire. One warm Spring morning, while she was still only a girl, in a green sheltered valley near the Tweed she heard a soft heart-breaking melody played by a young shepherd on his pipe. To this music she set her own words, thinking of the recent financial disaster which a number of local lairds had suffered and remembering also the old, sad defeat of the Scottish army in 1513 at the battle of Flodden and the death of the King:

> *'I've seen the forest adorned of the foremost,*
> *With flowers of the fairest, both pleasant*
> *   and gay;*
> *Full sweet was their blooming, their scent*
> *   the air perfuming,*
> *But now they are withered, and a' wede away'*

Buccleuch also plays host to the notorious Deacon **WILLIAM BRODIE** (*d* 1788), conman and burglar, whose two-faced lifestyle inspired one of Robert Louis Stevenson's greatest creations—*Dr Jekyll and Mr Hyde*. Brodie lies in an unmarked grave.

DEACON BRODIE
(after KAY)

Brodie was born in the Lawnmarket in Brodie's Close and became a successful cabinetmaker like his father. He rose quickly through the ranks of his craft and became a senior official in the Incorporation of Wrights and Masons—a 'Deacon'. By day he was courteous, respectable and dependable—but by night a different side of his personality emerged.

Brodie gambled secretly and lost large sums of money even though he cheated with loaded dice. And in 1787 the whole of Edinburgh was baffled by a series of daring and inexplicable burglaries. No one could understand how the thief could have gained entry and left no trace behind him.

What no one knew was that William Brodie, using the keys provided by his customers, made copies which would then be used for his moonlight activities.

At the dead of night Brodie and his gang slipped into the houses they had targeted, stole what they could and then departed as stealthily as they had come. He grew so bold that he actually let himself into a house during the day and walked past an old lady who had lost the power of speech, laughing in her face as he went about his business.

But on 5th March 1787 Brodie and his men tried to rob the Excise House in Chessel's Court. They succeeded but all they got was £16 in shillings and sixpences and a few stamps—they had missed £600 hidden in a secret drawer in the cashier's desk!

Not long after, lured by a reward and the promise of a pardon, one of Brodie's accomplices let the cat out of the bag and revealed just how the robbery had been committed and the identity of the culprits.

In due course Brodie's house was searched. A pair of pistols was found buried underneath the hearth and a further search revealed the other tools of his trade—iron wedges, an iron crowbar, a shaded lantern, false keys and picklocks.

The 'TOOLS' of BRODIE'S TRADE

Brodie was not to be caught easily. He managed to escape to the Continent and would have sailed off to America but for a careless slip which led to his arrest in a public house in Amsterdam.

He and one of his accomplices were sentenced to be hanged at the west end of the Luckenbooths (just outside the entrance to St Giles).

Brodie came out wearing an elegant black suit, his hair dressed and powdered. After praying with a minister, the two prisoners put on the white execution caps and the executioner tied their arms together. They climbed onto the newly-constructed platform, but Brodie found that the noose was on too short a rope. He jumped down and waited while the knots were adjusted. Once again he jumped up onto the platform, but still the rope was incorrectly knotted. Brodie got down *again*. Finally all was ready. He carefully took off his cravat, opened his shirt collar, button-ed up his waistcoat and coat and helped the executioner to fix the rope. He pulled the white nightcap down over his face and stood with folded arms, waiting.

His companion dropped his hand-kerchief as a signal and the table dropped away from both of them. The great bell of St Giles tolled as the execution took place. It was a few minutes before three.

Behind him Brodie left the following message: 'My neck now being about to embrace the halter, I would recommend it to all roughs, sharpers, thieves and gamblers whether in high or low station, to take care of theirs, by leaving off their wicked practices and becoming good members of society in future'.

THE FOLLOWING GRAVEYARDS
ARE NOT CENTRAL—
A MAP OF THE CITY AREA
AND TRANSPORT ARE ADVISABLE

COLINTON

Enter under the arch of the churchyard wall by the iron swing-gate. As you approach the bunched yew trees beside the church an iron mortsafe (grave security grill), brown with rust, stands at your left like some ancient armoured missile. Go down the left side of the church until you reach the back of the building. You may catch a faint hint of tobacco in the air. For as you reach the end of the church, a small temple with a pitched roof, barred with a blue iron grill, preserves the mortal remains of **JAMES GILLESPIE** (1725-97), whose name can be seen in the mosaic floor circled by a laurel wreath.

It was down at Spylaw in his snuff-mill that Gillespie worked, an old blanket over his shoulders and a night-cap on his head, like something out of a nursery-rhyme.

In their tobacco shop in the High Street, James and his brother John served many of the lawyers and literary figures of the time, including the poet Burns. Outside the shop was a wooden black boy holding a clay pipe, leaning on a barrel marked 'Tobacco'. Inside, Gillespie's snuff-grinder worked steadily away. Both artefacts can still be seen in Huntly House Museum.

Snuff was a popular habit in the eight-eenth century. It was pinched from a little hollow at the back of the hand, just below the thumb.

At his death James Gillespie left £12,000 to build a hospital for old men and women, and £2,700 to build a free school for poor boys. The hospital was built in Bruntsfield but demolished in 1870 and the income used instead to provide annual pensions. James Gillespie's School, after a long and honourable history as a fee-paying institution, is now a comprehensive school for boys and girls.

Gillespie had a rather prominent nose, (as can be seen from the marble bust in the entrance to James Gillespie's High School) and his commercial success produced the following verse at the sight of his fine carriage rattling over the cobbles: '*Wha wad hae thocht it, That noses had bocht it?*'

To the right side of the Gillespie tomb, look out for Dr **LEWIS BALFOUR** (1777-1860), Robert Louis Stevenson's grandfather, minister at Colinton. He is also buried in this cemetery.

GRANGE

You enter the gates of the cemetery from Grange Road, opposite the church of St Catherine's-Argyll. To your left outside the gates, beside the narrow Lovers Lane, is a dried-up drinking fountain set in the wall, a reminder of more leisurely and less sanitary days.

Once you are inside the cemetery turn hard right. Put any idea of ghosts out of your mind. The only unnatural night-time activity here is the mindless vandalism of those who push over headstones for fun in the dark.

Walk along the broad path running beside the wall which borders Grange Road as it changes into Beaufort Road. First impressions are of a place wide open to the skies, filled with gurgling pigeons— a place of peace.

Along this path to your right is a massive memorial to a spiritual giant, the Revd **THOMAS CHALMERS** (1780-

1847), the Anstruther-born leader of the 'Disruption' in the Church of Scotland.

He was born in Fife, the sixth child of a dyer and shipowner. He graduated from St Andrews University and was licensed as a preacher when only 19. Although he spent some time as a teacher of Mathematics at St Andrews he was ordained a minister in 1803.

Then one day Chalmers had a conversion experience. His skill as a preacher was transformed and congregations would assemble as much as four hours before a service just to hear him.

Henry Lord Cockburn, a close friend, describes Chalmers thus: 'It would not be difficult to find him ugly. But he is saved from this by singular modesty, kindness and simplicity of manner, a strong expression of calm thought and benevolence. The magic lies in the concentrated intensity which agitates every fibre of the man'.

His career as a minister reached a crisis point in 1843 when he and 470 other ministers left the Church of Scotland. They strongly believed that ministers should be appointed by local congregations and not by patrons as the law of the time demanded. This was the birth of the Free Church.

In 1845 Dr Chalmers became principal of the new Free Church College.

On 30th May 1847, Dr Chalmers

passed away quietly during the night and the next morning was found at peace with himself and the world.

Close by, guarded by two grey Celtic crosses, is the large flat monument to Dr Chalmers' friend **HUGH MILLER** (1802-56), a titanic figure in the worlds of science and religion—a true environmentalist.

Miller's brilliant mind was also his tragic downfall. Paranoia began to take the place of genius. He now carried a revolver in fear of being attacked. From time to him he experienced sharp stabbing pains in his head and he became obsessed with the idea that his brain was disintegrating, that he was going mad.

One morning his body was found on his study rug, a hole in his chest made by a bullet from his revolver. The revolver was found in the bath close beside him. Lying on the table was a sheet of paper with the message: '*Dearest Lydia, my brain burns. I must have walked and a fearful dream rises upon me. I cannot bear the horrible thought. God and the Father of the Lord Jesus Christ have mercy on me … farewell*'.

The postmortem discovered that Miller had been suffering from brain disease.

Further tragedy followed his death, however.

The revolver, rusted from lying overnight in Hugh Miller's bath, was taken to the gunsmith who had supplied it, in order to discover exactly how many bullets had been fired.

It was lunchtime when the gun was brought into the shop. It was handed over to the foreman **THOMAS LESLIE** with the warning, 'Mind, it is loaded'. Leslie examined the rusty safety-catch. He held it up to his eye. He lifted the hammer to count the bullets. At that instant the pistol went off through his eye, blowing his brains out.

Thomas Leslie, who had eight children and had worked with guns for 25 years, was buried in the Grange Cemetery earlier on the very same day as Hugh Miller.

To the left of Hugh Miller's grave is **THOMAS NELSON** (1780-1861) who founded the publishing firm of Thomas Nelson & Sons which made its name from the reissue of cheap editions of established authors. Next to him lies his son, also **THOMAS NELSON** (1822-92), who worked in the family firm and invented the rotary press in 1850, making high-speed printing possible.

ANDREW USHER (1826-98), a member of the famous Edinburgh brewing family, is buried here in the Grange. You can see his portrait in the entrance to the Usher Hall whose construction he made possible in 1896 with a gift of £100,000.

Look out also for Dr **THOMAS GUTHRIE** (1803-73), the great social reformer. Born in Brechin, Guthrie studied surgery and anatomy at Edinburgh, one of his teachers being the notorious Dr Robert Knox of Burke and Hare fame.

Guthrie then went to Paris for further study. What he saw there opened his eyes to the degrading poverty and the evil of which human beings were capable. This changed his life.

He received a licence to preach as a minister in 1825 and eventually took up a charge in Forfar. When the Disruption came Guthrie was one of the leaders of the Free Church. Installed in Free St John's in the West Bow in Edinburgh, he began a crusade for a system of 'Ragged Schools' which would provide shelter, training and education for the many young children who roamed the streets of the capital, learning the lessons of crime and brutality. Dr Guthrie was supported in his first *Plea for Ragged Schools* (1847) by Hugh Miller.

Look very carefully and you may be able to find the family grave of **DYER**. Here rests **ELIZABETH CULLEN CHANTRELLE** (née Dyer) (1851-78), the victim of one of the most heartbreaking murders the city has ever seen. Her name does not appear on the stone.

As a young girl of 15 she was sent to

school at the Newington Academy. There she met Eugène Marie Chantrelle, a 43 year old teacher. Over the following months a romance developed between the debonair, charming Chantrelle and his young pupil. Then she discovered she was pregnant and, against his will, Chantrelle was forced to marry her.

But Chantrelle had already grown tired of her. He treated her badly—swore at her, threatened and beat her. He went out with other women and flaunted these affairs in her face. Sometimes he locked her out of the house at night. Many times Elizabeth had to barricade herself from him at her mother's house. Twice she had to call in the police to protect her. After the fourth child had been born, she went to see a lawyer about a divorce. Only love for her children made her stay with Chantrelle. But the beatings continued. He even threatened Elizabeth with a pistol.

When his free-spending lifestyle led him into debt, he took out life insurance for £1,000 on his wife. But the policy would only pay out the lump sum if Elizabeth died accidentally. Chantrelle decided on murder, making up a mixture containing opium with which he poisoned his wife.

The police dismissed Chantrelle's claim that a gas leak had accidentally killed his wife when traces of opium were found in the victim's body. Eugène Chantrelle was found guilty of poisoning and hanged on Friday 31st May 1878. The crowds who came to the Calton Hill were disappointed. The only sign of his execution was the hoisting of the black flag.

Ironically on the other side of the wall which borders Lovers Lane is the grave of **MARY JANE PRITCHARD** (née Taylor) and her mother and father.

Mother of five children, Mary Jane was the victim of 'The Human Crocodile', Dr Edward Pritchard, who poisoned first his mother-in-law with tartarised antimony and then his 38 year old wife Mary Jane in Glasgow.

When his mother-in-law died in Edinburgh, Dr Pritchard callously came through from Glasgow to the funeral.

Later, as his wife lay in her coffin at her parents home at 1 Lauder Road, Dr Pritchard made a show of bending down to kiss the lifeless corpse.

But the police eventually became suspicious, exhumed the mother-in-law's body and found it full of antimony. Dr Pritchard was arrested and tried at the High Court in Edinburgh. He was found guilty of murder and hanged on 28 July 1895 in Glasgow's Jail square, the last public execution in the city of Glasgow.

WARRISTON

In sharp contrast to the manicured lawns
and colourful glass-houses of the Royal
Botanic Garden, turn right off Inverleith
Row down Warriston Gardens to the
jungles of Warriston Cemetery where popular myth advises the visitor to bring a
pith helmet, a machete, and carry an
elephant gun!

Go through the blunt stone pillars of
the main gate. Walk straight ahead down
the path for 143 paces to where the path
branches left and right like a wishbone.
Immediately in front of you as the ground
begins to slope down, you come to one of
the most pathetic sights in the graveyards
of Edinburgh—the tragic remains of the
famous 'Red Lady'.

The Red Lady is probably the strangest
and most magnificent of all Edinburgh's
graveside memorials—an arcaded Gothic
shrine of white marble and a roof of ruby-
coloured glass which bathed with light
the figure inside—a sleeping woman
MARY ANN ROBERTSON (1826-58),
daughter of Brigadier-General Manson of
the Bombay Artillery. Today, after an
outbreak of mindless vandalism, only the
stone foundations remain and a few chips
of the ruby glass.

JOHN MENZIES (1808-79), one of Britain's best-known stationers, is buried in Warriston. Educated at the Royal High School, Menzies served his apprenticeship in an Edinburgh bookseller before working in Fleet Street, London. He returned to Edinburgh in 1833 after his father's death and opened his own shop at the corner of Princes Street and Hanover Street.

Menzies bought the rights of the works of Charles Dickens and was an agent for *Punch* and *The Scotsman*. Later he opened a network of railway bookstalls, becoming one of the largest booksellers and stationers in the country.

ADAM BLACK (1784-1874) the publisher is also buried here. He was Liberal MP for Edinburgh and member of the Town Council. His premises were in the South Bridge and business prospered. He was able to buy the rights to the *Encyclopaedia Britannica,* to a number of Scott's novels and to involve himself in the publication of *The Edinburgh Review.*

Down a steep slope, surmounted by a large obelisk, is a grassy altar with a retaining wall—this is 'Simpsons' Slope', with its obelisk and the motto *'Nevertheless I live'*—the Simpson family burial-ground where Sir **JAMES YOUNG SIMPSON** (1811-70) lies, the pioneer of Anaesthetics.

Simpson's rise to fame came from an undignified fall under his dining-room table in 52 Queen Street, Edinburgh. Along with other doctors and assistants Simpson, by then Professor of Midwifery at Edinburgh, was experimenting on a number of substances which might help to make patients unconscious during medical operations.

After trying bottle after bottle of chemicals he picked up a container with chloroform it it. The doctors present each took a whiff and, in Simpson's words: 'immediately an unwonted hilarity seized the party. They became bright-eyed, very happy and very loquacious. The conversation was of unusual intelligence and quite charmed the listeners. But suddenly there was a talk of sounds being heard like those of a cotton-mill, louder and louder. A moment more, then all was quiet. And then—crash!' And thus the anaesthetic properties of chloroform were discovered.

Simpson founded the modern practice of Gynaecology and attended Queen Victoria at the birth of Prince Leopold. He was made a baronet in 1866.

PIERSHILL

Coming down the Portobello Road from Jock's Lodge, turn right after Northfield

Broadway outside the gates of Piershill Cemetery. Enter and walk 48 paces forward past the white war memorial to your left. A large white marble stone faces you, towering above the rest of the cemetery from the centre of a grassy mound. In one corner the stone is signed with a flourish: '*The Great Lafayette*' and on the flat stone below is the dedication—'*In memory of my dearest Beauty*'.

Stand quietly for a moment and feel the drama and excitement generated by this great theatrical performer, a wizard of deception and disguise, a romantic horseman and lion-tamer, a lover and trainer of performing dogs whose astonishing stage-show held audiences spellbound at the Empire Theatre in Nicolson Street in the spring of 1911. A man whose tragic and violent death stunned the city.

Immensely fit and highly intelligent, the 38 year old Californian **SIGMUND NEUBURGER** ('The Great Lafayette') (1873-1911) was a seasoned performer on the circuit of provincial theatres.

His speciality was dramatic illusion carried out under the stage name of 'The Great Lafayette' (named after the French general who defeated Britain during the American Revolution).

In May 1911 Neuburger was into the eighth month of a British tour and had already appeared for a week at the Empire Theatre, Edinburgh. In his second week 'The Man of Mystery' opened with a new feature, thrilling audiences twice-nightly with his dramatic illusion 'The Lion's Bride'.

It was the evening of Tuesday 11th May. 'The Lion's Bride' was approaching its climax. The theatre was crowded, the stage covered in elaborate Eastern scenery. Suddenly all the stagelights 'jumped' as if overloaded with current. An electric wire leading to a lantern fused. A small flame licked up into the scenery and in seconds a large piece hanging above the lantern caught fire. In moments a sheet of flame roared across the footlights, narrowly missing the orchestra. The safety-curtain fell, locking the fire into the backstage area. The audience left the theatre in an orderly fashion.

Meanwhile, behind the curtain, the fire was out of control. Lafayette ran back across the stage to search for a member of his company, shouting 'For God's sake, save yourselves!!' At that moment a large beam collapsed ...

The first casualties began to appear—a scene shifter badly burned, one of Lafayette's musicians unconscious from the effects of smoke, the theatre's fireman with a badly lacerated hand. By 3 am seven bodies had been found, only four of which could be identified. Of Lafayette, who had last been seen helping the members of his company to escape, there was no sign—and then a body was found.

The bodies of all the victims were taken to the police mortuary in the Cowgate and identified there by the Professor of Forensic Medicine. After the identification process was over what was thought to be Lafayette's body was taken to Glasgow and cremated.

Then, in an extraordinary turn of events, the real body of Lafayette was found in a hole on the stage, positively identified by the large diamond ring on his right hand and the double gold ring on his left.

The first body thought to be Lafayette had actually been Richards, a member of Lafayette's band, so identical in build that Lafayette used him as his double on stage.

Ironically Lafayette's dog 'Beauty', his faithful companion on and off stage for many years, given to him by the famous illusionist Harry Houdini, had died only the previous week and had already been buried at Piershill Cemetery. Lafayette's ashes were likewise borne to Piershill and laid to rest under a monument of Carrara marble, as he had requested only a few days before—beside his inseparable 'Beauty'.

Among the floral tributes was one from Houdini, his friend and previous owner of the dog.

Some months later rumours filtered back to Edinburgh of a new 'Lion's Bride' illusion being performed in America. But when the climax of the evening came, the actor in the lion's skin did not lift off his mask. Had The Great Lafayette performed the greatest illusion of all and survived the flames?

SELECTED
READING LIST

Anderson, P A, *Silences that Speak*, Edinburgh: Alex Brunton, 1931

Boyle, A, C Dickson, A McEwan, and C Maclean, *Edinburgh's Neglected Heritage*, Edinburgh: History of Science Unit, 1985

Willsher, B, *Understanding Scottish Graveyards*, Edinburgh: Council for British Archaeology Scotland, 1985